Assessment and Taxonomy of Child and Adolescent Psychopathology

DEVELOPMENTAL CLINICAL PSYCHOLOGY AND PSYCHIATRY SERIES

Series Editor: **Alan E. Kazdin,** *Western Psychiatric Institute*

In the Series:

Assessment and Taxonomy of Child and Adolescent Psychopathology

Thomas M. Achenbach

Volume 3.
Developmental Clinical Psychology and Psychiatry

SAGE PUBLICATIONS
Newbury Park   Beverly Hills   London   New Delhi

For information address:

SAGE Publications, Inc.
275 South Beverly Drive
Beverly Hills, California 90212

SAGE Publications India Pvt. Ltd.
M-32 Market
Greater Kailash I
New Delhi 110 048 India

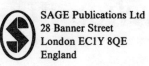

SAGE Publications Ltd
28 Banner Street
London EC1Y 8QE
England

Printed in the United States of America

Library of Congress Cataloging-in-Publication Data

Achenbach, Thomas M., 1940-
    Assessment and taxonomy of child and adolescent
psychopathology.

    (Developmental clinical psychology and psychiatry ;
v. 3)
    Includes index.
    1. Mental illness—Classification. 2. Mental
illness—diagnosis. 3. Child psychopathology.
4. Adolescent psychopathology. I. Title. II. Series.
[DNLM: 1. Mental Disorders—classification. 2. Mental
Disorders—diagnosis. 3. Psychopathology—in adolescence.
4. Psychopathology—in infancy & childhood.
W1 DE997NC v. 3 / WS 350 A117a]
RC455.2.C4A24   1985   616.89'0012   85-10798
ISBN 0-8039-2280-9
ISBN 0-8039-2281-7 (pbk.)

Second Printing

CONTENTS

Prototypes of Taxometry

INTRODUCTION TO THE SERIES

Interest in child development and adjustment is by no means new. Yet only recently has the study of children benefited from advances in both clinical and scientific research. Many reasons might explain the recent systematic attention to children, including more pervasive advances in research in the social and biological sciences, the emergence of disciplines and subdisciplines that focus exclusively on childhood and adolescence, and greater appreciation of the impact of such influences as the family, peers, school, and many other factors on child adjustment. Apart from interest in the study of child development and adjustment for its own sake, the need to address clinical problems of adulthood naturally draws one to investigation of precursors in childhood and adolescence.

Within a relatively brief period, the study of childhood development, child psychopathology, and child mental health has evolved and proliferated considerably. In fact, several different professional journals, annual book series, and handbooks devoted entirely to the study of children and adolescents and their adjustment document the proliferation of work in the field. Although many different disciplines and specialty areas contribute to knowledge of childhood disorders, there is a paucity of resource material that presents information in an authoritative, systematic, and disseminable fashion. There is a need within the field to present latest developments and to represent different disciplines, multiple approaches, and conceptual views to the topics of childhood adjustment and maladjustment.

The Developmental Clinical Psychology and Psychiatry Series is designed to serve uniquely several needs of the field. The series encompasses individual monographs prepared by experts in the fields of clinical child psychology, child psychiatry, child development, and related disciplines. The primary focus is on childhood psychopathology, which here refers broadly to the diagnosis, assessment, treatment and prevention of problems of children and adolescents. The scope of the series is necessarily broad because of the working assumption, if not demonstrated fact, that understanding, identifying, and treating problems of youth regrettably cannot be resolved by narrow, single discipline and parochial conceptual views. Commitment to the goal of understanding childhood disorders requires the sacrifice of professional parochialism. Thus, the series draws upon multiple disciplines and diverse views within any given discipline.

The task for individual contributors is to present the latest theory and research on various topics, including specific types of dysfunction, diagnostic and treatment approaches, and special problem areas that affect adjustment. Core topics within child clinical work are addressed by the series. Authors are asked to bridge potential theory and research, research and clinical practice, and current status and future directions. The goals of the series and the tasks presented to individual contributors are demanding. We have been extremely fortunate in recruiting leaders in the fields who have been able to translate their recognized scholarship and expertise into highly readable works on contemporary topics.

The present monograph, by Dr. Thomas M. Achenbach, addresses the topics of *Assessment and Taxonomy of Child and Adolescent Psychopathology*. The issues and advances encompassed by this book are fundamental to the investigation of all facets of developmental psychopathology. The present book provides a comprehensive presentation of alternative assessment and taxonomic procedures, underlying rationale, and current findings. The book is unique in its presentation of these alternative approaches in such an evenly balanced, thorough, incisive fashion and engaging style. Dr. Achenbach's own remarkable contributions to the field, already well known, make the text authoritative as well. The monograph addresses critical issues for the field and serve as the basis for evaluating specific disorders, assessment techniques, and overall strategies of research

—*Alan E. Kazdin, Ph.D.*
Series Editor

PREFACE

At first glance, this book may seem remote from the needs of troubled children and youth. Why bother with abstractions such as "taxonomy" and "cognitive economics"? These sound more like philosophers' hobby horses than tools of the clinician's trade.

If we already knew how to prevent or cure each disorder, there would be little need for a book like this. To advance our knowledge of causes and cures, however, we need a clear picture of the problems whose causes and cures are sought. To obtain such a picture, we need better assessment of individual cases and better taxonomic procedures for identifying the key similarities and differences between cases. To optimize assessment and taxonomy, we need to understand the strengths and limitations of the human minds that must ultimately use the data. An initial aim of the book, then, is to clarify aspects of human cognition that affect our understanding of psychopathology in children and youth. Thereafter, we will consider the cognitive economics of different approaches to assessment and taxonomy, developmental and metrical questions, and the taxonic integration of assessment data. By improving the standardized aspects of assessment and taxonomy, we can free human talents for aspects of clinical work that are not susceptible to standardization.

The book is intended for students and professionals in psychology, psychiatry, social work, and other fields concerned with maladaptive behavior in children and youth. It is oriented toward improving our understanding and practices rather than sanctifying the status quo. An expanding research base supports the proposed improvements, but the impact of the proposals will depend as much on the receptivity of practitioners as on new data.

In preparing this book, I have been greatly aided by extensive comments from Drs. Craig Edelbrock and Stephanie McConaughy, whose collaboration in related research also facilitates empirical testing of the ideas presented here. The related research is supported by grants from the W. T. Grant Foundation and the Spencer Foundation, for which I am most grateful. G. Dana Baron and Cathleen Gent have been of invaluable assistance in analyzing data, as well as in computer consultation and programming. Britta Müller has prepared the manuscript and its many changes with great patience. To Dr. Alan E. Kazdin go my thanks for being an admirably prompt and incisive editor.

—T.M.A.

1

THE COGNITIVE ECONOMICS OF CLINICAL THINKING

By way of introduction, let us consider some typical problems for which children and youth are referred for help.

Case #1

Linda, age 32 months, was referred to a child development clinic by her pediatrician for evaluation of lack of language development, resistance to toilet training, and disinterest in other children.

Linda's parents had first become concerned when she showed little sign of speech by the age of 2. After physical and hearing exams revealed no abnormalities, their pediatrician advised a wait-and-see attitude, as many children begin speaking normally after their second birthday. When Linda's speech still showed little progress, however, the pediatrician recommended a thorough developmental assessment, which was to include interviews with the parents, testing with the Gesell Scales of Infant Development (Knobloch & Pasamanick, 1974), the McCarthy Scales of Children's Abilities (1972), and a play session. Questions to be answered included the following:

(1) Is Linda mentally retarded?
(2) Does she have a specific abnormality of language?
(3) Is she emotionally disturbed or autistic?
(4) Are environmental or nutritional factors interfering with her development?
(5) Is she abused or deprived?
(6) What can be done to help now?
(7) What is the prognosis?
(8) What plans and expectations should be established?

Case #2

Robert, age 9, was brought to a child guidance clinic at the urging of a school psychologist. Although he was in the fourth grade, he was reading at a second-grade level. IQ was in the normal range, but he had never achieved as well as expected from his IQ. In the third grade he became disruptive in class and started fights on the playground. His fourth-grade teacher found his behavior intolerable, and he seemed to have no friends at school or at home. Questions included the following:

(1) Does Robert have a learning disability?
(2) Is he hyperactive?
(3) Does he have an attention deficit?
(4) Does he lack social skills?
(5) Should he receive one or more of the following: Medication? If so, what kind? Tutoring? Social skills training? Family therapy? Behavior modification? Psychotherapy?
(6) What is the prognosis?
(7) What long-term plans and expectations should be established?

Case #3

Judy, age 14, was taken to a private therapist by her mother, who was alarmed about her choice of friends, hints that she was smoking marijuana, declining school performance, crying spells, and poor eating and sleeping habits. Questions included the following:

(1) Is this a normal emancipation conflict?
(2) Will Judy become increasingly delinquent?
(3) Will her eating problems develop into anorexia nervosa?
(4) Is she depressed?
(5) Will her use of marijuana lead to serious drug abuse?
(6) What should be done now?
(7) How can she and her mother get along better?
(8) Should interventions be delayed until she is beyond the emancipation conflict?
(9) What is the prognosis?
(10) What long-term plans and expectations should be established?

Case #4

David, an 18-year-old high school senior, was referred to a community mental health center by his school counselor. After obtaining all As and Bs during his first two years of high school, his grades became erratic, dropping to D- in some subjects and remaining at the A and B level in others. Group ability tests over the years yielded IQ scores in the 130s and 140s. When asked about the low grades, David could give no explanation. He looked depressed, and one teacher reported an unprovoked temper outburst in class. Interviews at the community mental health center revealed suicidal thoughts, suspiciousness, and hints of experimentation with drugs, possibly phenylcyclidine (PCP). Questions included the following:

(1) Is David experiencing an adolescent identity crisis?
(2) How great is the risk of suicide?
(3) Is there an incipient psychosis?
(4) Will drug use continue?
(5) Is drug use a cause or a result of the other problems?
(6) Is David at risk for a drug-induced psychosis?
(7) Will David resume his progress toward college or withdraw from competitive achievement?
(8) What can be done to help now?
(9) What is the prognosis?
(10) What long-term plans and expectations should be established?

Despite marked differences in their ages and specific problems, these four cases share the following features that distinguish most child and adolescent disorders from adult disorders:

(1) It is not the "identified patients" who seek mental health services but others, such as parents, pediatricians, teachers and school counselors.
(2) The abnormalities involve failure to show expected developmental progress in areas such as speech, toileting, friendships, academic achievement, adaptation to the school culture, relations with family, and preparation for adulthood.
(3) Many of the problem behaviors are not intrinsically pathological, but are exhibited to some extent by most children and youth.
(4) Because most of the behaviors are not intrinsically pathological, decisions about what to do hinge on the prognostic implications of particular

problems: Which ones indicate deepseated disorders? Which ones are normal developmental problems?

(5) Interventions with children and youth should facilitate further development, rather than merely restoring a previous level of functioning, which is a typical goal for adults.

To choose the best form of help, we need to know the typical outcome for similar cases under various intervention and nonintervention conditions. The process of determining which cases are similar has two key facets:

- *Assessment*—identification of the distinguishing features of each case
- *Taxonomy*—the grouping of cases according to their distinguishing features.

These simple concepts are central to research, theory, and services pertaining to disordered behavior. Yet they are often obscured by confusion over how to select features that validly link each case to others like it. This confusion stems from problems in reducing a welter of clinical information to more manageable terms.

In dealing with psychopathology, we must weigh and combine diverse information. This can be viewed as a problem in what Mischel (1979, p. 741) calls *cognitive economics,* "the recognition that people are flooded by information which must somehow be reduced and simplifed to allow efficient processing and to avoid an otherwise overwhelming overload." Other complex endeavors also require efficient use of cognitive resources to avoid being overwhelmed with information. Yet the nature of child and adolescent psychopathology, the types of judgment required, and the level of our knowledge raise some unique issues.

By highlighting the information-processing tasks involved in understanding maladaptive behavior, I hope to elucidate not only the current status of assessment and taxonomy but also the possibilities for improvement. Although the focus is on the entire period of rapid development from birth to about age 18, the term "childhood" is used for convenience to include infancy and adolescence.

Views of childhood disorders are often dictated by concepts of adult psychopathology. Unfortunately, these concepts blur the differences between problems for which children and adults need help, differences in the relevant assessment data, and differences in developmental levels. Adult diagnostic categories, for example, have long shaped the study of childhood disorders. Yet the lack of entrenched diagnostic categories for childhood disorders may prove to be a blessing in disguise if it prompts use of better methodological and conceptual tools than were available when adult diagnostic constructs originated. Better ways of conceptualizing assessment and taxonomy can also improve child clinical research, which has suffered from confusion about the phenomena to be studied. In preparation for viewing assessment and taxonomy in light of cognitive economics, the remainder of this chapter will deal with aspects of human cognition that are heavily involved in clinical judgment.

PROBLEMS OF CLINICAL INFORMATION PROCESSING

Clinical assessment of adults relies mainly on interviews and tests, both medical and psychological. Assessment of children relies more on information from people other than the "identified patient," such as parents and teachers. With both children and adults, however, the clinician must elicit, process, remember, and integrate diverse data from the client and other sources. Clinical skill is often equated with the ability to predict behavior from a variety of data.

In a book entitled *Clinical Versus Statistical Prediction,* Paul Meehl (1954) contrasted two approaches to the prediction of behavior: *clinical or case-study prediction,* in which assessment data are mentally combined to formulate a diagnostic hypothesis from which to predict what is going to happen; and *actuarial or statistical prediction,* in which data are combined according to explicit rules that match the individual to cases for which outcome probabilities are known.

The two approaches do not necessarily differ in the initial data obtained—both methods can use self-reports, clinical observations, test findings, and demographic data, such as age and socioeconomic status. However, they differ fundamentally in how they use the data. In the clinical approach, data are mentally weighed and integrated to predict future behavior. In the actuarial approach, by contrast, data are combined according to rules that match the individual to other cases for which the distribution of outcomes is known.

The tables used to set life insurance premiums illustrate one form of actuarial prediction. These tables list current death rates for people classified by age, sex, and other variables, such as occupation and health history. The life insurance premium for a particular person is set according to the death rate for similar people. To set premiums, actuaries need not know the cause of every death. Nor does the agent who sells John Smith's policy make a clinical judgment of whether Smith will die in the next year. Instead, the tables must merely predict death rates accurately enough for insurance companies to maintain profitable but competitive premiums. This form of actuarial prediction does not generate prophecies about individuals, but statements of the proportion of a particular class of individuals who will show a particular outcome.

In another form of actuarial prediction, the outcome variable is not a categorical event such as death, but a quantitative score. College admissions officers, for example, combine applicants' high school grades and Scholastic Aptitude Test scores in a multiple regression equation that predicts each applicants' college grade average. The multiple regression equation is derived from relations between the predictor variables and college grade averages found for students in previous years. The admissions officers may impose a categorical cutoff, whereby they accept only those applicants who are predicted to have a passing grade average. However, the quantitative nature of the outcome variable also enables them to make finer-grained distinctions between more and less desirable candidates who are all above the cutoff.

Meehl (1954) compared the accuracy of clinical versus actuarial predictions of behavioral outcomes in areas such as the success of psychotherapy, various kinds of training, and parole from prison. He concluded that actuarial prediction was equal or superior to clinical prediction in nearly all cases, a conclusion borne out in subsequent research (Wiggins, 1981). We turn now to some findings on why clinical prediction is so difficult.

SOURCES OF BIAS IN HUMAN JUDGMENT

Cognitive research has uncovered biases that affect most human reasoning but are especially crucial in clinical assessment.

Illusory Correlation

Beginning with Chapman and Chapman (1967), research has shown that people processing information on a series of cases infer correlations between attributes that are not in fact correlated. This is called *illusory correlation*. In the Chapmans' study subjects viewed drawings and lists of symptoms attributed to the people who did the drawings. In reality, the symptoms were randomly paired with the drawings. Yet the subjects inferred that people who drew atypical eyes were suspicious and that men who drew muscular figures were worried about their masculinity. Similarly, after being shown Rorschach responses randomly paired with alleged attributes of the respondents, subjects in other studies inferred correlations between homosexuality and certain Rorschach signs. Clinicians inferred that these same signs were associated with homosexuality in Rorschachs they had seen, although research showed no association with homosexuality. Even when certain alleged attributes were *negatively* correlated with particular test responses, subjects still inferred positive correlations. Conversely, when other attributes were perfectly correlated with test responses, subjects failed to detect the correlations (Chapman & Chapman, 1971; Kurtz & Garfield, 1978).

Biased inferences of correlations seem to arise from the observers' own mental associations. However, explicit warnings to beware of illusory correlations have not prevented them, even with subjects who were skeptical of the psychological test they were judging (Kurtz & Garfield, 1978). Although preexisting assumptions spawn illusory correlations, failures to detect correlations that actually exist suggest a more fundamental problem, as discussed below.

Inability to Assess Covariation

Detection of "what goes with what" or *covariation* between attributes is a fundamental step in most sciences. It is also a goal of clinical training; by seeing a great many cases, we try to acquire an intuitive knowledge of covariation between important attributes. This knowledge of covariation should enable experienced clinicians to make more accurate assessments and predictions than inexperienced people. The evidence on illusory correlation suggests, however, that human beings are not very good at inferring covariation between attributes in a series of cases, even when the input data, definitions of attributes, and inferences are fairly simple.

Table 1.1 illustrates the problem of detecting covariation between two attributes in a series of cases. In this example the attributes are

TABLE 1.1
Reports of Bedwetting and Firesetting by Parents of
100 Clinically Referred 8- and 9-Year-Old Boys

		Wets the Bed	
		Yes	*No*
Sets	*Yes*	Cell A N = 6	Cell B N = 19
Fires	*No*	Cell C N = 14	Cell D N = 61

SOURCE: Achenbach and Edelbrock (1981).
NOTE: Pearson correlation = .02, not statistically significant.

bedwetting and firesetting, which are easily judged as present versus absent and which have been inferred to be associated (e.g., Freud, 1932). To keep the situation simple, consider only bedwetting and firesetting among 8- and 9-year-old boys seen in outpatient mental health services, as shown in Table 1.1. A Pearson correlation of .02 indicates no statistically significant association between the two problems. Other empirical studies have also reported no general association between bedwetting and firesetting (Heath, Hardesty, Goldfine, & Walker, 1983; Kuhnley et al., 1982), although bedwetting may be elevated among certain subsets of firesetters (Heath, Hardesty, & Goldfine, 1984).

If empirical studies indicate that bedwetting and firesetting do not tend to cooccur, why was an association between them inferred? Cognitive research shows that people often infer a substantial association between two attributes in a series of cases having a distribution similar to those shown in Table 1.1. This is because cases having both attributes (Cell A) are more salient than those in Cells B, C, and D, even though all cells are equally important aspects of the relation between two attributes.

As an example, when given cases distributed as shown in Table 1.2, people were asked to estimate the association between attributes X and Y on a scale ranging from 0 (for no association) to 100 (for perfect association). Their average estimate was 54. Yet the actual association was 0, because attribute Y was twice as likely to occur whether attribute X was present or not (Cell A versus B = 12 versus 6; Cell C versus D = 6

TABLE 1.2
Distribution of Attributes X and Y in Experiment
by Arkes, Harkness, and Biber (1980)

| | | Attribute Y | |
		Yes	No
Attribute X	Yes	Cell A N = 12	Cell B N = 6
	No	Cell C N = 6	Cell D N = 3

NOTE: Association between X and Y = 0

versus 3). People do not always make the same kinds of mistakes, however, because their estimates of covariation are affected by such factors as the labeling of attributes, the salience of particular combinations of attributes, and the difficulty of keeping both attributes in mind from case to case (Arkes & Harkness, 1983).

It is hard to judge the actual covariation between two behavior problems categorized as present versus absent, but most clinical judgments of covariation are far harder, as discussed next.

Attributes That Vary in Degree

Many attributes are perceived in degrees rather than categorically as present versus absent. To infer covariation, we must judge quantitative variations in such attributes. Consider, for example, inattentiveness and unhappiness, as scored in the three degrees shown in Table 1.3. Could we mentally keep track of even three degrees of these two attributes in 100 cases? And then intuitively infer the covariation indicated in the nine cells of Table 1.3? As found for 2×2 tables, cases having high scores on both attributes (Cell A) would be especially salient, even though the other eight cells are equally important in determining the actual degree of association.

Quantitative variation in attributes raises an additional problem: Unless the covariation between the attributes is perfectly positive or perfectly negative, what should we expect about their cooccurrence in particu-

TABLE 1.3
Reports of Inattentiveness and Unhappiness by Parents of
100 Clinically Referred 8- and 9-Year-Old Boys

| | | Unhappy, Sad, or Depressed | | |
		very true or often true	somewhat or sometimes true	not true
	very true or often true	Cell A N = 10	Cell B N = 14	Cell C N = 32
Can't Concentrate, Can't Pay Attention for Long	somewhat or sometimes true	Cell D N = 4	Cell E N = 16	Cell F N = 12
	not true	Cell G N = 1	Cell H N = 4	Cell I N = 7

SOURCE: Achenbach and Edelbrock (1981).
NOTE: Pearson r = −.04, not statistically significant.

lar children? For example, if X correlates .50 with Y in 100 cases, what is the likely magnitude of Y in a child who shows a high degree of X? Practical applications of quantitative associations between variables require more rigorous procedures than most people can employ intuitively.

Attributes Assessed in Different Ways

Many problems occur mainly in a single context, such as the home, school, or neighborhood. Others, such as learning disabilities, may have pervasive effects but can be pinpointed only through standardized testing. Clinical assessment requires multiple sources of data that differ in form, completeness, reliability, and validity. Most information from parents, for example, is obtained in face-to-face interviews, whereas information from teachers often is obtained through written comments. Information from standardized tests is conveyed via scores and interpretive reports. Depending on the child's age and a host of other variables, our direct contacts with the child may or may not be very informative. An interview, for example, may yield good examples of the problem

TABLE 1.4
Reports of Inattentiveness and Unhappiness by Teachers of
100 Clinically Referred 8- and 9-Year-Old Boys

		Unhappy, Sad, or Depressed		
		very true or often true	somewhat or sometimes true	not true
Can't Concentrate, Can't Pay Attention for Long	very true or often true	Cell A N = 14	Cell B N = 20	Cell C N = 23
	somewhat or sometimes true	Cell D N = 3	Cell E N = 13	Cell F N = 18
	not true	Cell G N = 2	Cell H N = 2	Cell I N = 5

NOTE: Pearson r = .13, not statistically significant.

behaviors, a clear statement of the child's perspective on the problems, rich symbolism for interpretation, or nothing of clear relevance to the reported problems.

Detection of covariation between attributes is hindered by differences in the nature, source, reliability, and validity of the data from which we draw inferences. Certain types of data, such as an IQ score, are obtainable in only one way, such as from a standardized test. However, clinically important problems are reported by different people in different contexts. Because the important people in a child's life often have different opportunities and standards for judging the child, perfect agreement is rare. This means that the reported intensity and covariation of behaviors depend on the source of the reports.

As an example, Table 1.4 shows teachers' ratings of inattentiveness and unhappiness on the same three-step scale as the parents' ratings in Table 1.3. Although some problems are observed only by parents or by teachers, inattentiveness and unhappiness can be observed by both parents and teachers. By comparing Tables 1.3 and 1.4, we see that parent and teacher reports differ not only in the scores for each item, but also in the resulting correlations between the items. To infer the covariation between these two problems, whose reports should we use? What should we do if we have reports from only one informant or differing

TABLE 1.5

Reports of Inattentiveness and Unhappiness by Parents of
100 Nonreferred 12- and 13-Year-Old Girls

		Unhappy, Sad, or Depressed		
		very true or often true	*somewhat or sometimes true*	*not true*
	very true or often true	Cell A N = 0	Cell B N = 2	Cell C N = 2
Can't Concentrate, Can't Pay Attention for Long	*somewhat or sometimes true*	Cell D N = 1	Cell E N = 5	Cell F N = 15
	not true	Cell G N = 0	Cell H N = 7	Cell I N = 67

NOTE: Pearson $r = .28$, $p < .01$.

confidence in reports from two informants? Could we intuitively infer the different patterns of covariation shown in Tables 1.3 and 1.4?

Even if we used trained observers, we would often find real differences in the intensity and covariation of behaviors at home and school, owing to differing environmental constraints. It is therefore important to assess the intensity and covariation of important behaviors as they are seen in different contexts, such as the home and school.

Assessment of Multiple Attributes

Covariation among multiple attributes is usually more important than covariation between pairs of attributes. Syndromes and other higher-order patterns consist of multiple attributes, which, in turn, may be associated with particular age levels, competencies, and family characteristics. The difficulty of clinically assessing covariation is greatly compounded when multiple attributes must be tracked, remembered, and judged in relation to one another. When the attributes vary from one situation to another, it is especially necessary to use quantitative methods rather than deriving higher-order patterns by intuition alone.

Generalization of Covariation from One Group to Another

Table 1.3 indicates that parents' ratings of inattentiveness and unhappiness are not mutually associated among clinically referred 8- and 9-year-old boys. Can we therefore assume the same lack of association between these attributes among children in general? Unfortunately not, because referred boys of other ages, nonreferred boys, and girls might show other patterns. Table 1.5, for example, shows different distributions and correlations of scores for nonreferred 12- and 13-year-old girls than for the 8- and 9-year-old boys shown in Table 1.3. (Note that even though there are 10 boys and no girls in Cell A, there is a significant positive correlation between the attributes for the girls but not the boys.) Inferences about two attributes in a caseload including these two groups are apt to miss the difference in correlations. Failure to recognize limits on the generalizability of observations leads to another source of bias, as discussed next.

The Representativeness Heuristic

Heuristics are strategies or rules for solving problems. They help us organize and simplify information, but they may also bias our judgment (Kahneman, Slovic, & Tversky, 1982). The representativeness heuristic may especially affect clinical judgments of the following types:

(1) Is it likely that Child A has Disorder X?
(2) Is it likely that Behavior A is caused by Condition X?
(3) Is it likely that Process X will result in Outcome A?

When answering such questions, people often evaluate the probabilities according to the degree to which they perceive A as being representative of X, in the sense of being typical of X. Hyperactivity, for example, has been regarded as typical of children with minimal brain dysfunction (MBD). Labeling of Robert (Case 2 at the beginning of the chapter) as hyperactive might therefore bias us toward diagnosing him as MBD on the basis of weaker evidence than we would demand for other inferences. Conversely, if we know a child has suffered brain damage, we may predict hyperactivity rather than other outcomes viewed as less representative.

Clinical judgment can be greatly aided by firm evidence on the actual relations between variables A and X. If associations between hyperactivity and MBD are well documented, for example, this information should certainly be used. Where such evidence is weak or inappropriately applied, however, reliance on the representativeness heuristic may make us insensitive to the factors discussed below.

Insensitivity to Base Rates

If the base rate (actual prevalence) of MBD in a population is 0, then viewing hyperactivity as representative of MBD would always lead to wrong judgments about the presence of MBD in hyperactive members of that population. To take a less extreme example, 85% of 6- and 7-year-old boys seen for outpatient mental health services were described by their parents with the questionnaire item "Can't sit still, restless, or hyperactive." The same item was reported for 32% of nonreferred 6- and 7-year-old boys (Achenbach & Edelbrock, 1981). Teachers reported this item for 67% of referred 6- and 7-year-old boys and 44% of nonreferred 6- and 7-year-old boys. Is it likely that the actual prevalence of MBD is as high as either 67-85% of referred boys or 32-44% of nonreferred boys?

Although the lack of a good independent criterion for MBD prevents us from knowing the actual prevalence, let us suppose that the prevalence is as high as 10% among nonreferred boys and 30% among referred boys. Even if hyperactivity were truly a sign of MBD and MBD were this common, we would be wrong more often than right if we always inferred MBD from reports of hyperactivity by parents or teachers, who are regarded as essential informants for hyperactivity (American Psychiatric Association, 1980).

Insensitivity to Sample Size

In another misuse of the representativeness heuristic, people often overestimate the degree to which a small sample is representative of a larger population. It may be forgivable for someone ignorant of statistics to generalize observations on a few cases to all children. It is less forgivable, however, when people who should know better are especially excited by a large correlation when it is found in a small sample, as in "Look! A correlation of .67 with only 9 subjects!" It is often forgotten that the smaller the sample, the less representative it is likely to be of the parent population. Consequently, chance correlations that are much larger than the true population correlation are more likely to be found in small samples than large samples.

This misapplication of the representativeness heuristic reflects confusion over the fact that a stronger relation between variables is required to reach a particular level of significance (e.g., p = .05) in a small sample than in a large sample. Thus, with a sample size of 9, a Pearson correlation must be at least .67 to be significant at p = .05. This means that sample sizes of 9 are potentially so unrepresentative of their parent populations that the sample correlation has to be at least .67 before we can be 95% confident that the population correlation exceeds zero. In a sample of 100, however, we need a correlation of only .19 to be 95% confident that the population correlation exceeds zero. As evidence that a population correlation exceeds zero, then, a correlation of .67 in a sample of 9 is only as impressive as a correlation of .19 in a sample of 100!

Insensitivity to Predictability

When informed of the current status of something, such as a person's performance in one situation, people tend to take this information as representative of future status. When they do, their predictions often are insensitive to the unreliability of the evidence and to its lack of bearing on future status (Tversky & Kahneman, 1974). Excessively favorable or unfavorable interview impressions lead to predictions of exceptionally good or bad outcomes, despite the fact that the interview impressions may be neither reliable nor in any way related to the outcome variable.

The Availability Heuristic

One of the presumed strengths of clinical judgment is its ability to bring a wealth of experience to bear on each new case. As we become acquainted with a child and family, for example, we may be reminded of another case. The mental availability of previous cases may be affected by such factors as vividness, recency, intensity of involvement with the case, or similarities of physical appearance, mannerisms, names, family constellation, parental occupation, and so on. Or the matching may be with a vivid pattern described for someone else's case or for a particular type of disorder.

Although mental pattern-matching is essential for applying knowledge, readily available patterns may inappropriately shape our judgment of new cases. This fosters the "disease of the week" and "medical student's disease," whereby learning about a disorder primes us to see it everywhere (even in ourselves). It also explains the illusory correlations discussed earlier: Available associations cause us to infer correlations where none exist.

Mental availability may accurately reflect certain phenomena, but the availability heuristic can also cause systematic errors of judgment, such as the following (Tversky & Kahneman, 1974):

(1) It can cause us to miss the ways in which a new case differs from other cases it superficially resembles.

(2) It can cause us to match a case to an easily remembered pattern, despite greater similarity to a less available pattern.

(3) It can lead us to infer correlations where none exist.

(4) It can bias our estimates and predictions to reflect events most vivid to us rather than most representative of what is to be estimated or predicted.

The Confirmatory Bias

Several lines of research show that mental hypothesis testing is biased by an excess weighting of data that tend to confirm our beliefs, to the neglect of other types of data (Arkes & Harkness, 1983). In the process of simplifying input in order to draw inferences, it certainly makes sense to seek data consistent with the hypothesis being tested. Because it is so hard to be perfectly even-handed with confirmatory and contradictory data, however, the confirmatory bias can lead to erroneous acceptance of hypotheses. Hypotheses formed early in a clinical evaluation, for example, may be too readily accepted because we continually seek evidence to confirm them. (When a hypothesis owes its privileged status to being thought of first, this is also known as a *primacy bias*.)

Research on predictions made from case-study materials has shown not only that early hypotheses are retained as the data increase, but that confidence in the predictions increases greatly, even though their accuracy does not (Nisbett, Zukier, & Lemley, 1981; Oskamp, 1965). Our confidence in our predictions may thus exceed their accuracy at the end of an extensive diagnostic work-up more than at the beginning, when confidence is realistically low. Furthermore, experienced clinicians have been found more susceptible to the biasing effects of initial information than nonclinicians, who had much less confidence in their judgments than did the clinicians (Friedlander & Phillips, 1984).

OVERCOMING BIASES

The preceding list of biases in human judgment may make clinical assessment seem like an impossible task. It is a tribute to human ingenuity, however, that such biases are detected and documented. In fact, one of the greatest strengths of the human mind is its ability to invent methods for overcoming our limitations. Our lack of biological equipment for breathing under water, flying, and space travel has been surmounted by the building of some amazing machines. Limitations on our attention span, memory, and information-processing abilities have been surmounted by devices ranging from simple tabulations to computers. Such techniques can expand the power of clinical judgment by facilitating information-processing tasks for which human minds are ill-suited. Human abilities can thus be freed for judgments that are not possible in other ways, for forming therapeutic alliances with clients, and for tailoring therapy to the needs of the individual child and family.

As we consider various approaches to assessment and taxonomy in Chapters 2 through 4, we will evaluate them in terms of their vulnerability to information-processing biases. In Chapters 5 and 6, we will consider ways in which assessment and taxonomy can be better adapted to helping troubled children and youth.

SUMMARY

To find the best means for helping children and youth, we need to know the typical outcome for similar cases under various intervention and nonintervention conditions. There are two key facets to the determination of similarity between cases: (1) *assessment*—identification of the distinguishing features of each case; and (2) *taxonomy*—the grouping of cases according to their distinguishing features.

For valid assessment and taxonomy, we must organize disparate information into meaningful wholes. This can be viewed in terms of cognitive economics—ways of reducing and simplifying what would otherwise be an overwhelming flood of information. A better understanding of how human information processing affects clinical assessment can help us determine the most appropriate means and goals for assessment. This, in turn, can improve the tailoring of treatment to individual needs.

There is abundant evidence that actuarial procedures for weighting and combining assessment data yield more accurate predictions than does mentally combining data. However, rather than rejecting clinical judgment as hopelessly inaccurate or actuarial methods as impractical, it is necessary to strengthen the contributions of both approaches by understanding obstacles to the effective use of clinical information.

Human judgmental biases arise from sources such as the following: *illusory correlation*—the inference of correlations between attributes that are not actually correlated; *inability to assess covariation*—the inability to determine the degree of association between attributes observed across a series of cases, which is especially hard when attributes vary in degree, are assessed in different ways, involve higher-order patterns, or are generalized from one group to another; the *representativeness heuristic*—incorrectly viewing a limited sample as representative of a larger class, which often involves insensitivity to base rates, sample size, and predictability; the *availability heuristic*—the excessive influence of salient mental associations on observations, inferences, and predictions; and the *confirmatory bias*—weighting confirmatory data more heavily than data inconsistent with our hypotheses.

The detection of biases is a tribute to the human mind, which is especially adept at inventing ways to overcome its own limitations. By improving aspects of clinical information processing that are hard for the unaided human mind, we can devote human abilities more fully to the aspects of assessment and treatment for which they are most essential.

2

MAJOR ASSESSMENT PARADIGMS

In Chapter 1 we considered certain problems in the cognitive economics of clinical thinking. In this chapter we will consider the ways in which different assessment paradigms deal with these problems.

A *paradigm* is a conceptual model for organizing ideas and information. The history of science suggests that paradigms shape scientists' choices of problems for study, the methods they choose, and their interpretations of findings (Kuhn, 1970, 1977). Paradigms also shape clinical activity, often in more subtle ways than scientific activity, which emphasizes explicit testing and revision of assumptions.

By structuring thought in terms of certain assumptions, variables, and methods, scientific and clinical paradigms deflect attention from alternative conceptions. Yet without paradigms, neither scientific nor clinical activity would have a clear focus. Objectives would be poorly defined, efforts would be scattered, and knowledge would not be cumulative. To make proper use of paradigms, we should be aware of the ways in which they both facilitate and limit our understanding of disordered behavior. To illustrate the impact of different paradigms, we will consider four that are especially relevant to child psychopathology. These are the medical, psychodynamic, psychometric, and behavioral paradigms, which will be discussed in terms of their origins, current status, and key questions. We will then consider their strengths and vulnerabilities with respect to the information-processing biases outlined in Chapter 1.

THE MEDICAL ASSESSMENT PARADIGM

Origins

This paradigm grew out of nineteenth-century medical science. The success of biomedical research in identifying organic etiologies for many illnesses fostered a view of mental disorders as disease entities, each one caused by a specific abnormality of the brain (Griesinger, 1845). According to the medical paradigm, the purpose of assessment (or diagnosis) is to infer an underlying organic abnormality from observable signs and symptoms. Each distinctive syndrome is assumed to reflect a particular organic condition. The observable aspects of the disorder are thus regarded as clues to biological variables that define the disorder.

The medical assessment paradigm played a vital role in rescuing the study of disordered behavior from demonology and superstition. Through systematic documentation of symptom patterns, physical correlates, course, and outcome, it achieved an important success with one disorder in particular—general paralysis, later called *paresis* (i.e., "incomplete paralysis"). Progressively better descriptions of symptoms culminated in the 1840s with a definition of paresis in terms of a combination of mental symptoms, such as memory loss and irrationality, with physical symptoms, such as motor impairment, usually ending in death. Once the definition of the syndrome was standardized, biomedical research from the 1840s through the 1870s revealed inflammation in the brains of many people who died of paresis. Possible causes for the inflammation were gradually narrowed to syphilitic infection, which was confirmed experimentally in 1897 by Krafft-Ebing's demonstration that innoculation with syphilis did not produce secondary symptoms in paretics—because they were already infected. In 1906, the success of the Wassermann test in detecting syphilis in paretics made it an important addition to medical assessment of mental disorders.

Current Status

The medical assessment paradigm has been successful in identifying organic correlates of disorders that have then been traced to specific organic etiologies. This is true of several forms of mental retardation, including cretinism—caused by thyroid deficiencies; Down syndrome and Klinefelter syndrome—each caused by an extra chromosome; and phenylketonuria—caused by a genetically based intolerance for phenylalanine, a substance present in many foods.

In its contemporary form, the medical assessment paradigm employs interviews and physical examinations to detect signs and symptoms that help the clinician form hypotheses about a disorder. These hypotheses are then tested through further questioning, examination, laboratory tests, X-rays, and so on. In the assessment of behavior disorders, psychological tests are used to detect abnormalities of perceptual-motor, cognitive, and emotional functioning, in a fashion analogous to laboratory tests. Ultimately, however, the various kinds of data are mentally combined by the clinician to diagnose a specific disorder in each child. The goal of assessment is thus to determine which disorder explains the child's problems.

Disorders Without Known Organic Etiology

Beside disorders for which organic etiologies are known, disorders of unknown etiology are often interpreted in terms of the medical assessment paradigm. Some of these seem more like organic disorders than others. Infantile autism, for example, starts so early in life and involves such marked deviance from normal development that the medical assessment paradigm seems to be an appropriate conceptual model. This does not necessarily mean, however, that all aspects of the disorder can be understood from this perspective. Even if a specific organic etiology is found, the distorted cognitive, behavioral, and social-emotional development of autistic children requires detailed assessment from perspectives other than those of the medical paradigm. The same may be true for psychotic disorders that emerge later in childhood, where the degree and nature of the deviance suggest a disease-like condition, but where our lack of knowledge of the specific etiology and the need for multifaceted help necessitate other forms of assessment as well.

Hyperactivity

Certain less extreme disorders have also been interpreted in terms of the medical assessment paradigm. Hyperactivity (or Attention Deficit

Disorder with Hyperactivity), for example, has long been blamed on brain dysfunction. Historically, one source of the assumed link between hyperactive behavior and brain dysfunction was the observation of uncontrolled activity in children struck by an epidemic of encephalitis in the 1920s. A second source was the discovery that stimulant drugs seemed to reduce overactivity in disturbed children (Bradley, 1937).

Perhaps the most influential historical source was the work of Strauss, Lehtinen, and Werner during the 1930s and 1940s. Comparing normal children, brain-damaged retarded children, and retarded children thought to be undamaged, they concluded that brain damage caused distractibility, which could be detected with perceptual-motor tests (Strauss & Lehtinen, 1947).

As a result of these findings, the terms *Strauss syndrome* and *MBD* became synonymous with a behavioral syndrome composed of distractibility, hyperactivity, impulsivity, short attention span, emotional lability, poor perceptual performance, and clumsiness. Some workers have also used the term MBD synonymously with LD (learning disability) and SLD (specific learning disability; e.g., Ochroch, 1981). Beside behavioral and perceptual-motor problems, MBD is thought to be indicated by "soft" (i.e., equivocal) signs of neurological dysfunction, borderline electroencephalograms (EEGs), and developmental histories suggestive of brain trauma.

The use of interviews, physical examinations, perceptual-motor tests, and developmental histories to infer MBD as the cause of hyperactivity made it a prototypical application of the medical assessment paradigm to common behavior problems. During the 1970s, hyperactivity was publicized more than any other childhood disorder and became routinely treated with stimulant drugs.

Yet several studies show that hyperactivity is not usually a symptom of brain damage. Preschool children known to be brain damaged, for example, have not been found more hyperactive than normal preschool children (Ernhart, Graham, Eichman, Marshall, & Thurston, 1963). Although the brain-damaged preschoolers performed poorly on psychological tests, they had deficits in all areas, not just perceptual-motor functioning.

A study of children immediately after they received head injuries showed that behavior problems increased only after severe injury (indicated by amnesia of at least seven days duration) and that the behavior problems did not follow uniform patterns like those imputed to MBD (Brown, Chadwick, Shaffer, Rutter, & Traub, 1981). Soft neurological signs and nonfocal EEG abnormalities are also dubious grounds for diagnosing MBD in hyperactive children, as they are quite common in nonhyperactive children as well (Boll & Barth, 1981).

Beside MBD, other organic abnormalities have been proposed to account for hyperactivity. These include neurotransmitter abnormalities (Wender & Wender, 1978), abnormal arousal levels (Zentall & Zentall, 1983), food sensitivities (Feingold, 1976), food allergies (Trites, Ferguson, & Tryphonas, 1978), developmental delays (Buchsbaum & Wender, 1973), and constitutionally determined extremes of cognitive style and activity level (Kinsbourne & Swanson, 1979). Although there is evidence that several of the hypothesized organic abnormalities are associated with hyperactivity in some children, none of them seems to account for many clinical diagnoses of hyperactivity.

It is possible that an organic etiology will eventually be found for hyperactivity and associated attention deficits. Yet, unlike autism and psychotic conditions, the troublesome behaviors are not intrinsically pathological. Instead, they differ mainly in degree from behavior shown by most children at some time in their development. Furthermore, children's activity and attentional problems vary markedly from one situation to another and are often mixed with a variety of other problem behaviors. Viewing hyperactivity and attentional deficits as symptoms of organic abnormalities may therefore prematurely foreclose more comprehensive assessment of children's functioning.

Depression

In adults, manic-depressive ("bipolar") disorders are characterized by extreme alternation between irrational euphoria and deep depression. The apparent lack of environmental causes for these shifts, familial patterns suggestive of genetic influences, and the efficacy of drug therapy have supported the application of the medical assessment paradigm to adult manic-depressive disorders.

Prior to about 1930, there were reports of conditions resembling manic-depressive disorders in a few children (Kasanin & Kaufman, 1929). From the 1930s through the 1960s, however, interest in childhood depression gave way to the psychoanalytic view that true depressive disorders could occur only after the superego was fully internalized in adolescence.

The success of drug therapies for adult affective disorders in the 1960s rekindled the quest for depression in children. A few cases of childhood manic-depressive disorders were again reported, and their apparently favorable response to lithium therapy lent credence to the medical assessment paradigm for such disorders in children (DeLong, 1978). Efforts to apply the medical assessment paradigm to less extreme affective problems in children have been more problematic. In an influential study, for example, Weinberg, Rutman, Sullivan, Penick, and Dietz (1973) reported that 63 percent of prepubertal children seen at an educational clinic were suffering from a "depressive illness." Children were diagnosed depressed if they showed dysphoric mood (unhappy, irritable, hypersensitive, or negative) and self-deprecatory thoughts, plus at least two of the following: aggressive behavior, sleep disturbance, change in school performance, diminished socialization, change in attitude toward school, loss of usual energy, unusual change in appetite and/or weight. Inferences of "depressive illness" were based on a pediatric neurologist's informal interviews with the children and their parents. These were backed up by interview-based reports of greater improvement in children who received antidepressant medications than in children for whom medication was recommended but not given. No standardized assessment of symptoms was reported; treatment conditions were neither uniform nor blindly evaluated; and there were no placebo controls.

Despite the dubious data base, the concept of depressive illness in children was soon broadened even beyond the Weinberg et al. criteria. *Masked depression,* for example, was inferred from aggressive, hyperactive, and other problem behavior that is used defensively "to ward off the unbearable feelings of despair" (Cytryn & McKnew, 1979, p. 327). Other authors inferred masked depression from psychophysiological reactions, truancy, running away, sexual promiscuity, and fire setting (see Kovacs & Beck, 1977).

The concept of masked depression was subsequently rejected (Kashani, Husain, Shekim, Hodges, Cytryn, & McKnew, 1981), and efforts have been made to assess childhood depressive disorders with a combination of psychometric, interview, and biological indices, such as the dexamethasone supression test (DST). Widely used in research on adult depression, the DST involves administering dexamethasone and then recording blood cortisol levels during the following day. Elevated cortisol levels have been found in very few children or adolescents who were not diagnosed as depressed but in 20 to 40 percent who were diagnosed as depressed (Burke, McCauley, Mitchell, & Smith, 1983; Klee & Garfinkel, 1984). The association with depression is thus far from perfect and may reflect other abnormalities, such as weight loss. Much more research is required to test the relations between organic and other indices of diagnostic constructs such as depressive disorders in children and adolescents.

Key Questions

The interpretation of diverse behaviors as symptoms of illness raises the following questions about use of the medical assessment paradigm for childhood disorders of unknown etiology:

(1) How can we decide which problem behaviors are symptoms of "illness" and which ones are transient developmental phenomena, reactions to situational stress, personality characteristics, or nonorganic disorders?

(2) How can we decide when affects such as unhappiness are normal reactions to life events versus abnormal conditions?

(3) How can we decide whether a particular affect is a cause or an effect of behavioral problems? Hyperactivity and aggression, for example, can earn children negative consequences that may make them feel unhappy, rejected, anxious, or worthless. Although these affects may then be of concern in their own right, we would be wrong to view hyperactivity and aggression as symptoms of an affective illness in such cases.

THE PSYCHODYNAMIC ASSESSMENT PARADIGM

Origins

Psychodynamic theory originated in response to organic medicine's failure to explain hysterical symptoms. The patterns of dysfunction seen in hysterical paralyses and anesthesias, for example, defied basic anatomical principles. Building on work by Pierre Janet and Josef Breuer, Sigmund Freud in the 1890s theorized that such symptoms stemmed from the repression of unacceptable thoughts. According to Freud, the emotional excitation associated with the repressed thoughts remained active and could be *converted* into a somatic form causing bodily dysfunctions. Freud therefore called such disorders *conversion hysterias.*

By getting patients to engage in free association—to say whatever came to mind—Freud pieced together the repressed thoughts. He could then help patients gain insight into the unconscious meaning of their mental associations. This allowed the repressed thoughts and affects to become conscious which, in turn, was expected to relieve the symptoms.

As the psychodynamic paradigm evolved, free association remained the prototypical assessment technique, but it was joined by a host of other approaches to the unconscious mind. Freud (1900) himself added the interpretation of dreams as an assessment technique. In children too young to free associate, Anna Freud (1936) interpreted play, dreams, and reactions to emotional events as clues to unconscious impulses and the defenses against them.

Another psychodynamic approach was to use ambiguous stimuli to evoke responses interpreted as projections of the unconscious mind. Beginning in the 1900s with Carl Gustav Jung's word association tests and Hermann Rorschach's inkblots, projective techniques continue to be widely used (Lubin, Larsen, & Matarazzo, 1984). Beside words and inkblots, projective tests include pictures for which subjects make up stories, such as the Thematic Apperception Test (TAT; Murray, 1943) and Children's Apperception Test (CAT; Bellak & Bellak, 1974); incomplete sentences for which subjects supply endings (e.g., Rotter & Rafferty, 1958); and drawing techniques, in which subjects' drawings of people, houses, and trees are interpreted as reflecting unconscious thoughts and feelings. Psychodynamic assumptions also guide most clinical interviewing and therapy oriented toward the detection and interpretation of thoughts, feelings, and defenses.

Current Status

In contrast to the medical assessment paradigm, the goal of psychodynamic assessment is not to pinpoint a specific disease. Instead, the goal is to detect unconscious motives, conflicts, fixations, regressions, personality structures, and defenses, which are then used in an *idiographic* formulation of the case. (*Idiographic* refers to detailed portrayal of the individual as a unique entity, in contrast to *nomothetic,* which refers to general laws pertaining to all individuals.) The focus is on a network of inferred constructs that define the individual's personality and explain his or her behavior. Psychodynamic assessment thus epitomizes what Meehl (1954) called "clinical" or "case study" prediction.

Most psychodynamic constructs originated in Freud's theory, but their meanings changed as the theory developed. They are subject to varying interpretations, and few have been operationally defined. Although there are reliable measures of certain psychodynamic variables, such as anxiety, these measures focus on nomothetic constructs rather than on inferred variables that vary from person to person (e.g., Glennon & Weisz, 1978; Reynolds & Paget, 1981; Spielberger, 1973). An anxiety measure that compares a person's responses with those of a normative group may not contribute much to a psychodynamic assessment of the sources of anxiety, conscious versus unconscious levels, defense mechanisms, and so on.

Projective tests—such as the Rorschach, TAT, and figure drawings—typify psychodynamic efforts to obtain idiographic portraits of personality. Certain nomothetic systems for scoring projective tests have achieved adequate reliability for variables such as color and movement responses to the Rorschach (Exner & Weiner, 1982) and unusual features of human figure drawings (Koppitz, 1968). Nomothetic Rorschach scores have been found related to outcomes for seriously disturbed children (Tuber, 1983), and scores for human drawings have been related to gender disturbance in children (Zucker, Finegan, Doering, & Bradley, 1983). There is little evidence, however, that personality dynamics can be reliably inferred from projective tests (see Achenbach, 1982; Gittelman, 1980). There is also little evidence that important personality variables can be reliably inferred from psychodynamic interviews, even during the full-scale psychoanalysis of adults, where conditions should be optimal (Auerbach & Luborsky, 1968; Garduk & Haggard, 1972).

Key Questions

The difficulty of drawing reliable inferences from projective tests and psychodynamic interviews raises the following questions about the psychodynamic assessment paradigm:

(1) How can we obtain reliable data on which to base complex psychodynamic inferences about the functioning of individuals?

(2) If reliable data can be obtained, how can we determine what factors are conscious versus unconscious, which ones are causes versus effects, and which ones reflect motives versus structures versus defenses?

(3) How can we use idiographic portrayals of personality to identify similarities among cases that will help to improve our choice of treatment and predictions of outcome?

THE PSYCHOMETRIC ASSESSMENT PARADIGM

Origins

Whereas the medical and psychodynamic paradigms originated with efforts to understand pathological conditions, the psychometric paradigm originated with efforts to measure psychological traits, especially intelligence. This initially involved extrapolating nineteenth-century evolutionary biology to psychological functioning. Darwin's cousin, Francis Galton, for example, hypothesized that intelligence is an innate and unitary trait that contributes to the survival of the fittest. Galton also hypothesized that innate intelligence should be measurable in terms of sensory-motor performance. During the 1880s, he devised numerous tests of sensory-motor functioning, such as perceptual acuity, reaction time, and tapping speed. He also devised statistical techniques for analyzing the results. His student, J. McKeen Cattell, brought psychometrics to the United States and coined the term "mental test."

Galton's construct of intelligence as a unitary trait measurable via sensory-motor tests did not gain much empirical support. His tests did not correlate well with one another or with other presumed measures of intelligence, such as teachers' ratings and academic grades (Bolton, 1891; Sharp, 1898; Wissler, 1901). Yet by applying measurement procedures to behavior via objectively scored tests and statistical analysis, Galton laid the foundations for the psychometric paradigm. Despite the failure of his construct of intelligence, the psychometric paradigm was soon applied more successfully to the assessment of academic ability and a host of other variables.

Use of a Practical Validity Criterion

Taking a more pragmatic approach than Galton, Alfred Binet and Theophile Simon (1905/1916) sought to identify children whose abilities were retarded enough to require special education. Binet and Simon were not committed to any theory of the nature, source, or immutability of intelligence. Instead, they sought reliable and valid measures of the cognitive processes actually used in school. They therefore devised test items requiring the kinds of judgment and reasoning expected in school, without requiring academic skills such as reading and writing.

To validate their items, Binet and Simon assessed the items' correlation with practical indices of academic functioning, such as grades, school progress, and teachers' judgments. Scores on the tests were soon found to be more reliable than teachers' ratings (Kuhlmann, 1912). Contemporary editions of the Binet test still retain the original items, such as naming common objects; copying a square; putting together two halves of a bisected rectangular card; and solving logical problems (Terman & Merrill, 1973).

The Normative-Developmental Approach

Beside selecting tasks to tap academically important cognitive processes, Binet and Simon departed from Galton's approach in another important way. Instead of trying to quantify intelligence in absolute terms, they took a *normative-developmental* approach. This meant selecting items for their sensitivity to the normal growth of children's abilities. An item was retained only if the percentage of children passing it increased steadily with age. Items were then grouped according to mental age (MA) level, defined as the first age at which a majority of normal children passed them. For example, an item that was passed by increasing percentages of children at ages 4 through 7, with 6 years being the first age at which a majority passed it, was assigned to the 6-year MA level.

According to the normative-developmental approach, performance was not evaluated in terms of an *absolute* level of ability, but *relative* to the performance of normative groups of agemates. The judgment of a child's ability was thus based on the child's performance compared to other children of the same age. Binet and Simon initially decided that children needed special education if their MA was more than two years below their chronological age (CA). However, a two-year lag reflects proportionally more retardation at young ages than at older ages. A *ratio* of MA to CA (the IQ score) was therefore adopted that remains constant if a child's rate of cognitive growth remains constant, as compared to that of normal peers.

Most ability tests, including the current edition of the Stanford-Binet, have since dropped the MA/CA ratio in favor of IQ scores that represent a child's standing in terms of standard deviation units from the mean of normative samples of agemates. The normative-developmental approach is likewise used in tests of infant development, achievement, and perceptual-motor functioning, as well as in developmental screening measures, such as the Minnesota Child Development Inventory

(Ireton & Thwing, 1974). However, it is much less evident in psychometric assessment of psychopathology, to which we now turn.

Psychometric Assessment of Psychopathology

The Minnesota Multiphasic Personality Inventory (MMPI) is a prototypical application of the psychometric paradigm to psychopathology. In developing the MMPI, Hathaway and McKinley (1943) started with a large pool of items expected to elicit different responses from people diagnosed as having different disorders. Most of the items are self-referent statements, such as "At times I feel like smashing things." Other items imply values, such as "Most people make friends because friends are likely to be useful to them." Respondents mark each item as true, false, or cannot say.

To construct MMPI scales, the candidate items were administered to mental patients who had received different diagnoses, such as schizophrenic, manic, and psychopathic (now designated as "antisocial personality"). Items were retained if they evoked different responses from different diagnostic groups or if they were thought to serve other functions, such as indicating lying, defensiveness, ego strength, or masculinity versus femininity. Clinical scales were then constructed from items found to characterize a particular diagnostic group, such as schizophrenics. The items were also administered to normal adults, and cutoff points for distinguishing between the normal and clinical groups were established at two standard deviations above the mean of the scores obtained by the normals.

Although individual clinical scales, such as the manic scale, were expected to bear a one-to-one relation to particular diagnoses, it was found that particular *profiles* of scale scores were more closely associated with certain diagnoses than were individual scales. Profiles elevated on both the Psychopathic deviate (Pd) and Manic (Ma) scales, for example, were more characteristic of people diagnosed psychopathic than were profiles elevated on the Pd scale alone (Dahlstrom, Welsh, & Dahlstrom, 1972).

Norms and profile configurations have been developed for adolescents (Marks, Seeman, & Haller, 1974), but the MMPI's use with children and early adolescents is limited by its length (566 items), its focus on adult diagnostic categories, and the morbid, sexual, and adult content of many items. In an effort to extend the MMPI approach to children, Wirt and Broen (1958) constructed the Personality Inventory for Children (PIC). The general format and true-false response alternatives are similar to the MMPI, but the PIC differs from the MMPI in two basic ways:

(1) Lacking well-established diagnostic categories on which to target the PIC, Wirt and Broen wrote 50 items to cover each of the 11 areas that they deemed important, including withdrawal, excitement, reality distortion, aggression, somatic concern, anxiety, social skills, family relations, physical development, intellectual development, and asocial behavior.

(2) The respondent is not the person who is being assessed, but the mother of the child whose personality is being assessed.

These departures from the MMPI also characterize other efforts to assess child psychopathology, owing to a lack of well-established diagnostic categories, children's inability to provide reliable data in a standardized fashion, and the importance of parents' reports. In lieu of diagnostic categories against which to validate PIC items, the authors constructed scales in several ways, such as having clinicians nominate items to measure predetermined constructs and choosing items that empirically discriminated certain criterion groups, such as delinquents (Wirt, Lachar, Klinedinst, & Seat, 1977). Interpretive statements were then derived from characteristics found to correlate with the scale scores of children seen at a particular clinic (Lachar & Gdowski, 1979).

Beside the multiscale approach of the MMPI and PIC, the psychometric paradigm has been applied to the assessment of single-trait constructs, such as anxiety and depression. Some of the measures are self-report scales, such as the Children's Manifest Anxiety Scale (Reynolds & Paget, 1981) and Children's Depression Inventory (Kovacs, 1981). Others are designed for scoring observations of children's behavior under specified conditions, such as the Preschool Observation Scale of Anxiety (Glennon & Weisz, 1978).

Psychometric procedures have also been applied to projective stimuli designed to assess psychodynamic constructs. The Blacky Test (Blum, 1960), for example, consists of cartoons of disguised psychosexual conflicts, such as castration fears represented by a picture of a puppy about to have its tail cut off. Children choose from multiple-choice answers intended to reflect different psychodynamic constructs. Like most psychometric assessment of adult psychopathology, the measures designed for children tend to treat their target variables as developmentally static, without separate scales for different ages.

The basic principles characterizing these various psychometric approaches can be summarized as follows:

(1) Both the administration and scoring of the assessment procedures are standardized according to explicit rules.
(2) Multiple items are used to assess target traits, with each item serving as a sample of a trait domain.
(3) A quantitative score is obtained for each trait.
(4) The meaning of individual scores depends on a nomothetic framework of normative and criterion group data.
(5) Scores indicate how an individual compares with a particular reference group.

Key Questions

The psychometric assessment paradigm is an outgrowth of "trait theories," which are less oriented toward causal explanation of disordered behavior than are the medical and psychodynamic paradigms that we considered earlier. Rather than postulating particular causal mechanisms, the psychometric paradigm provides a general methodology for identifying important individual differences in functioning, without much concern for the precise causes of these differences. This raises the following questions:

(1) As the psychometric paradigm is not based on a theory of the cause or nature of maladaptive behavior, how should we decide what to assess with it?
(2) How can psychometric assessment take account of developmental differences in behavior disorders?
(3) How can we integrate psychometric data with other types of data to form a comprehensive picture of individual children and their life situations?

THE BEHAVIORAL ASSESSMENT PARADIGM

Origins

The medical, psychodynamic, and psychometric paradigms originated with efforts to explain behavior in terms of hypothetical constructs. The behavioral assessment paradigm, by contrast, originated largely with John B. Watson's (1913) proposal that human behavior could be explained entirely in terms of observable stimuli and responses. This approach was based on Bekhterev, Pavlov, and Thorndike's demonstrations of control over animal behavior via conditioned stimuli, without inferences about underlying organic or mental variables.

In applying behavioral principles to maladaptive behavior, Watson argued that most fears resulted from the pairing of neutral stimuli with aversive experiences, as illustrated in case studies of children's fears (Jones, 1924; Watson & Rayner, 1920). From the 1920s to the 1950s there were sporadic reports of behavioral treatments, but they were not widely applied to clinical disorders until the 1960s.

The renaissance of behavioral treatment was led by Joseph Wolpe's (1958) *reciprocal inhibition* therapy, which inhibits anxiety by reinforcing benign responses in the presence of the anxiety-provoking stimuli. The most widely used form of reciprocal inhibition is *systematic desensitization*. The first step in systematic desensitization is to list everything that makes the client anxious, ranked in order from most to least anxiety arousing. The *anxiety hierarchy* (as the rank-ordered list is called) is then divided into thematic categories, and the client ranks the items within each category. Thereafter, the client is taught to relax while being helped by the therapist to imagine stimuli from the anxiety hierarchy. The process of desensitization starts with the least threatening stimuli in the hierarchy. When these no longer evoke anxiety, the therapist helps the client relax while imagining stimuli higher in the hierarchy.

Although hypnosis was originally used to help clients imagine the anxiety stimuli, hypnosis is now omitted in many cases. With children, for example, *in vivo* desensitization is often used, whereby the child is gradually exposed to the feared stimuli while being rewarded for making nonanxious responses.

By focusing on the specific stimuli and responses to be treated, Wolpe helped to launch the behavioral assessment paradigm. Other behavioral approaches, such as operant conditioning, stress the need for direct assessment of problem behavior in its real-life context, in preference to clients' verbal reports. The direct assessment of behavior continues during treatment to determine whether the desired changes actually take place and remain stable. Behavioral assessment is thus viewed as an intrinsic component of treatment, rather than as preceding and separate from treatment.

Principles of Behavioral Assessment

As behavioral methods proliferated, behavior modifiers drew the following contrasts between behavioral assessment and "traditional" medical, psychodynamic, and psychometric assessment (Mash & Terdal, 1981):

(1) Whereas traditional assessment focuses on inferred constructs, behavioral assessment focuses on the maintenance of behavior by the current environment.

(2) Whereas traditional assessment assumes that behavior is consistent across situations, behavioral assessment assumes that behavior is situationally determined.

(3) Whereas traditional assessment views the persistence of behavior as a function of internal causes, behavioral assessment views it as a function of consistency in the environment.

(4) Whereas traditional assessment views responses as clues to underlying attributes, behavioral assessment views responses as samples of relevant behavior.

(5) Whereas traditional assessment seeks to diagnose an underlying condition and judge its prognosis, behavioral assessment seeks data that will directly guide treatment.

(6) Whereas traditional approaches assess behavior in clinical settings, behavioral assessment seeks observations of behavior in its natural environment.

(7) Whereas traditional assessment is a separate process that precedes treatment, behavioral assessment is a continuous process integrated into treatment.

Applications of Behavioral Assessment

Gerald Patterson (1980) has made some of the most ambitious applications of behavioral assessment to children's behavior disorders. Patterson's trained observers record the behavior of children in their homes in terms of categories such as "Cry," "Ignore," "Noncomply," "Tease," "Whine," and "Yell." Because assessment focuses not only on the child's behavior but also on the environmental contingencies supporting it, observers must record the behavior of everyone who interacts with the child. The conditional probabilities for sequences of stimuli and responses are then computed to identify the contingencies affecting the child's behavior.

Patterson's work represents a tour de force of behavioral assessment that requires trained observers to make extensive observations of multiple family members on repeated occasions. Two or more observers are needed to check reliability. Elaborate statistical analyses are also needed to identify the antecedents and consequences of each child's problem behaviors. Yet even these extensive efforts can sample only a small subset of problem behaviors in exceptionally cooperative families. Furthermore, Patterson has found that the observed contingencies explain only a small proportion of the children's problem behaviors.

Although direct behavioral assessment also includes more convenient methods, such as tests of avoidance of feared stimuli, surveys show that behavioral clinicians do not adhere closely to the ideals of behavioral assessment in their practices (Swan & MacDonald, 1978; Wade, Baker, & Hartmann, 1979). Instead, many use traditional methods, such as interviews and tests, doubtless due to the cost and impracticality of having trained observers record behavior in its natural environment. The hope that behavioral assessment would avoid the reliability and validity problems of traditional assessment has not been fulfilled either. As Patterson (1981, p. viii) points out, the traditional problems of "validity, stability of behavior over time, bias, the effects of observer presence, and normative data" may be especially difficult for behavioral assessment to solve.

One of the key innovations of behavioral assessment—its emphasis on the specificity of behavior—may also be a "two-edged sword," as Kazdin (1979) calls it. If we assume that behavior is truly specific to the situation in which it occurs, then we cannot draw conclusions about behaviors and situations inaccessible to our observations. We would therefore ignore many important problems, such as stealing, vandalism, attempted suicide, and sleep disruption. We would also be unable to generalize from observations of behavior in one situation to situations that are not observed. Furthermore, if we assume that each type of behavioral response is specific, we cannot effectively assess covariation among behaviors that may reflect syndromes or other higher-order groupings (Kazdin, 1985).

One response to the difficulty and limitations of direct behavioral assessment has been *multimethod behavioral assessment* (Nay, 1979). As applied to children, the multiple methods include interviews, standardized tests, checklists and log books completed by parents, observations in clinical as well as natural settings, and tests of responses to simulated problem situations. Yet these multiple methods must also contend with the "traditional" problems of reliability, validity, representativeness, generalizability, and norm referencing. Furthermore, they must contend with another problem initially skirted by behavioral assessment: the problem of *aggregating* diverse and often contradictory data about individual children in *standardized* ways that link children needing similar forms of help (Mash, 1985).

Key Questions

The ideals and methods of behavioral assessment have greatly advanced the empirical documentation of problem behavior, the linkage of assessment to treatment, and our awareness of the effects of environmental contingencies. Nevertheless, to make better use of behavioral assessment, we need to address the following questions:

(1) How can we relate the specific behavior of a particular child assessed in a particular situation to knowledge accumulated on similar children assessed in other times and places?

(2) How can we assess behaviors that are refractory to direct assessment because they are covert, affected by direct assessment, infrequent, or scattered over diverse situations?

(3) How can we detect patterns of behavior that may be more appropriate targets for change than molecular responses taken one by one?

THE COGNITIVE ECONOMICS OF ASSESSMENT PARADIGMS

The major assessment paradigms differ in their origins, their objectives, the types of information they seek, and the ways in which they process information. They also differ in their vulnerabilities to the information-processing biases that we considered in Chapter 1. Table 2.1 summarizes the sources of bias most likely to affect each of the major paradigms, as discussed next.

Illusory Correlation

Biases involving illusory correlation may especially affect medical and psychodynamic assessment when conclusions about covariation are

TABLE 2.1
Sources of Information-Processing Biases in Major Assessment Paradigms

	Paradigms			
Sources of Bias	Medical	Psychodynamic	Psychometric	Behavioral
Illusory correlation	where clinical observations are the data base	reliance on clinical observations as a data base	—	—
Inability to assess co-variation	where clinical observations are the data base	lack of operational definitions	—	situational specificity
Representativeness heuristic	disease concept	idiographic fallacy	nomothetic fallacy	lack of principles for linking cases
Availability heuristic	vivid cases	vivid cases	favored assessment methods	favored treatment methods
Confirmatory bias	assumption of organic abnormalities	assumption of unconscious determinism	—	assumption of environmental determinism
Other limitations	premature closure	problems of testability	lack of causal hypotheses	premature closure

based on clinical observations. Such observations are an important source of hypotheses, but accurate conclusions about correlations require systematic tabulation and quantitative analysis of attributes across many cases. Although tabulation and quantitative analysis have become common in medical research on physical illness, medical and psychodynamic inferences about behavior disorders often imply correlations that may well be illusory, as illustrated in Chapter 1.

The psychometric paradigm is less likely to be affected by illusory correlation because the basic data are tabulated and analyzed quantitatively. The behavioral paradigm is also less likely to be affected because it does not seek to identify correlations between attributes observed across cases.

Inability to Assess Covariation

Inability to assess covariation between attributes is especially apt to affect psychodynamic assessment because psychodynamic variables are seldom defined operationally. Behavioral assessment uses operational definitions, but does not usually assess covariation among behaviors. Where clinical observations form the data base, the medical paradigm is vulnerable to inability to assess covariation, but this can be overcome by assessing covariation through tabulation and quantitative analysis of operationally defined attributes. The psychometric paradigm specifically emphasizes assessment of covariation through quantitative analysis of operationally defined attributes.

The Representativeness Heuristic

The representativeness heuristic affects all four paradigms, but in very different ways. The medical paradigm implies that signs of deviance are representative of a particular underlying disease. Such an assumption may short circuit efforts to understand the specific determinants of each behavior in its own right. If we assume, for example, that hyperactivity is typical of brain damage or that unhappiness represents a depressive illness, we may neglect the many possible situational and developmental determinants of these "symptoms." This may be justified if we have a well-validated diagnostic test for a disease, but there is little evidence that most behavior disorders involve diagnosable physical disease. We should not, therefore, subordinate the assessment process to unvalidated disease concepts. Even if disease concepts are ultimately validated for some disorders, they are unlikely to account for all the associated maladaptive behaviors for which help is needed.

In psychodynamic assessment, the biasing effect of the representativeness heuristic stems largely from the idiographic use of constructs such as id, ego, superego, drives, defense mechanisms, and unconscious conflicts. Psychodynamic theorists have explained the putative association between enuresis and firesetting, for example, in terms of these constructs (Freud, 1932). Despite the lack of empirical support for an actual correlation between enuresis and firesetting (discussed in Chapter 1) and the difficulty of reliably assessing the psychodynamic constructs, an idiographic personality portrait was held to represent a general class of enuretic firesetters.

Psychodynamic assessment is unequaled in its efforts to understand the individual's thoughts, feelings, and motives. This potential strength of psychodynamic assessment is perverted, however, by construing an idiographic picture of unverified constructs as literally representative of the individual's functioning across time and situations or as representative of a class of similar people. We must therefore avoid the *idiographic fallacy* of extrapolating unvalidated psychodynamic conceptions of the individual personality to situations or people for which there is no empirical validation.

The psychometric paradigm's vulnerability to the representativeness heuristic stems from a tendency opposite to that of the psychodynamic paradigm. Whereas psychodynamic assessment may unduly extrapolate from individuals to people in general, psychometric assessment may unduly extrapolate from group findings to the individual case. An example of this *nomothetic fallacy* would be the assumption that a person who has the MMPI profile associated with diagnoses of hysteria has all the characteristics reported for hysterics. This would be unjustified, because the statistical associations between MMPI profiles and clinical diagnoses are far from perfect, even in the research samples in which they were originally obtained. Thus, even if a statistically significant association is found between a particular MMPI profile and diagnoses of hysteria in a research sample, not everybody having the profile would be independently diagnosed as a hysteric and not everybody diagnosed as hysteric would have the profile.

Unreliability in both the MMPI and clinical diagnoses limits the correlation between them. Furthermore, even if they were both perfectly reliable and valid measures of exactly the same diagnostic construct, not every feature of hysteria occurs in everyone who is validly diagnosed as hysteric.

Nomothetic generalizations are also limited by differences between research samples in which statistical associations are obtained and the characteristics of individual clients. For example, interpretive statements for particular scores on the Personality Inventory for Children (PIC) are based on statistical associations obtained on children seen in an inner-city Detroit clinic (Lachar & Gdowski, 1979). Without cross-validation in samples differing in such characteristics as ethnicity and socioeconomic status, however, it is hard to know how accurately the interpretations would apply to a child from a very different background.

Different interpretations are sometimes made from the same nomothetic scores on an individual, even when automated procedures avoid the idiosyncracies of individual clinicians and their personal knowledge of a case. Dahlstrom et al. (1972), for example, showed that interpretations of a single MMPI profile by different computer scoring firms produced very different impressions of a client. Some of the differences were due to different formats (e.g., a series of descriptive adjectives versus descriptive paragraphs) and differences in the cautions with which interpretations were qualified. However, there also were major differences in emphasis on the severity of pathology indicated by particular scale scores and in the scale scores that were considered in the interpretation. Such inconsistencies illustrate the risk of bias when nomothetic data are applied to individual clients, even where the interpretations are automated and the data are as extensive as those for the MMPI. Proper use of automated interpretation thus requires rigorous standards for applying nomothetic data to individual assessment (Matarazzo, 1983; Turkington, 1984).

Theoretically, the behavioral paradigm should not be vulnerable to the representativeness heuristic, because it need not generalize from individuals to groups or from groups to individuals. As McFall (1982) points out, however, behavioral assessment cannot avoid the problem of representativeness by restricting itself to molecular response units in specific situations. The choice of units itself involves an assumption that they are representative of important aspects of a client's functioning. "Out of seat" and "off task" behavior, for example, may be chosen as easily observed problem behaviors, but they are not necessarily representative of a child's overall pattern of problem behavior. For some children, these behaviors may be good indices of inattention in the classroom, whereas for others they may be incidental byproducts of aggression (e.g., getting out of seat to hit other children). For still others, they may be responses to obsessional thoughts or hallucinations. It is therefore important to determine the relations among different problem behaviors in a particular child, both within and across situations.

To evaluate behavioral interventions and choose the best intervention for a particular problem, we need to aggregate molecular data in terms of response classes, types of disorders, types of clients, or types of problem situations. Without clear principles for aggregating molecular data, behavioral assessment is vulnerable to the representativeness heuristic when behaviorists extrapolate from the specific to the general or from the general to the specific, as they inevitably must.

The Availability Heuristic

All four assessment paradigms can be biased by overreliance on highly salient or "available" cognitive patterns. In medical and psychodynamic assessment, judgments of a case may be unduly shaped by memories of another case that was similar with respect to presenting complaints, family constellation, and the like. Salient patterns may also stem from particularly vivid cases seen either personally or reported by someone else. Although mental pattern-matching is a key step in applying previous experience, excessive reliance on the most available patterns can obscure important differences between new cases and the patterns to which we match them.

Psychometric and behavioral assessment depend less on mental pattern-matching than do medical and psychodynamic assessment. Reliance on our favorite psychometric procedures, however, can have an effect like the availability heuristic in medical and psychodynamic assessment. If we rely exclusively on a particular test, for example, we may view all cases according to the scales of that test, even if it neglects certain crucial variables. Similarly, reliance on a particular behavioral procedure selectively highlights certain features while obscuring those that require other approaches. If we assess social anxieties solely via anxiety hierarchies, for example, we may neglect a child's tendency to evoke other people's hostility, which will be a continuing source of anxiety. Although assessment seldom is restricted to a single method, it is important to recognize how our favorite concepts and methods shape our judgments of individual cases.

The Confirmatory Bias

When we assume that we know the cause of a problem, we overweight data that confirm our assumptions (Arkes & Harkness, 1983). Confirmatory biases are most likely to affect assessment based on paradigms that make strong causal assumptions. This is true of the medical paradigm, which assumes causation by organic abnormalities; the psychodynamic paradigm, which assumes causation by unconscious psychological determinants; and the behavioral paradigm, which assumes environmental determinants. Because human minds are less able to use disconfirming than confirming data, adherents of a particular paradigm may be insensitive to input that violates their causal assumptions. This can both bias their judgment of individual children and prevent them from appreciating the contributions of other paradigms.

The psychometric paradigm's lack of intrinsic causal assumptions makes it less vulnerable to confirmatory biases than are the other paradigms. Some workers hold causal assumptions about particular psychometrically defined traits, however, such as genetic determination of intelligence test performance. This could spawn a confirmatory bias in the interpretation of test scores, but it should not affect the scores actually obtained on properly administered tests.

Other Limitations

Beside vulnerability to biases, each paradigm has other limitations. The psychometric paradigm's lack of causal hypotheses reduces its vulnerability to confirmatory biases, but also limits its potential for explaining behavior disorders. It mainly contributes methodology that can be applied to a wide variety of assessment objectives.

Whereas the psychometric paradigm is oriented toward maximizing the reliability and validity of assessment, the psychodynamic paradigm offers a wealth of clinical concepts and assumptions but few methods for testing them. Efforts to test psychodynamic theory have been hampered by problems in operationally defining the target variables, obtaining reliable assessment data, and deriving testable hypotheses (see Achenbach, 1982, chap. 9). Studies failing to support psychodynamic theory have been criticized for interpreting the theory too simplistically, but the nature of the paradigm makes empirical tests difficult.

A limitation shared by the medical and behavioral paradigms is that their commitment to particular causal explanations may lead to premature closure in conceptualizing a child's needs. This refers not just to the effect of the confirmatory bias on etiological inferences but to views of the child as a patient to be cured versus a healthy organism to be taught more adaptive behavior. Such differences can lead to very different professional behavior toward children and families, which in turn affects their attitudes toward their own problems. Although all assessment communicates certain attitudes and expectations, medical and behavioral assessment may especially promote premature closure on the part of clients as well as practitioners.

SUMMARY

Paradigms are conceptual models for organizing ideas and information. In the medical paradigm, underlying organic abnormalities are inferred from observable signs and symptoms. This paradigm fostered the scientific study of mental disorders in the nineteenth century and led to the discovery of physical causes for a variety of disorders. However, applications of the medical paradigm to common childhood problems of unknown etiology, such as overactivity and depressed affect, raise the following questions: How can we decide which problems are signs of illness and which are not? How can we decide which affects are normal reactions to life stress and which are not? How can we decide whether an affective problem is a cause or an effect of a behavior problem?

The psychodynamic paradigm has implicated a host of psychological variables in disorders such as hysteria that have not been explained by the medical paradigm. Its goal is idiographic portrayal of personality and psychopathology. Applications to children raise these questions: How can reliable psychodynamic inferences be made? How can judgments of relations among the various idiographic attributes be made? How can we identify similarities among individuals on which to base treatment and prediction?

The psychometric paradigm is mainly a source of methodology that can be applied to many facets of children's functioning. It has yielded reliable and valid cognitive measures that employ a normative-developmental approach to comparing children with normative samples of agemates. Applications of the psychometric paradigm to assessment of childhood disorders raise the following questions: As the paradigm does not have a causal theory, what should be assessed? How can psychometric assessment take account of developmental differences in the patterning of behavior disorders? How can psychometric data be integrated with other types of information?

The behavioral paradigm attempts to avoid problems of "traditional" assessment by focusing on the situationally specific behaviors to be altered. This has improved documentation of children's behavioral problems and has linked assessment more closely to treatment. Behavioral assessment faces many of the same problems as other forms of assessment, however, and raises the following questions: How can we aggregate situationally specific behaviors to build knowledge of particular types of problems and children? How can we assess behaviors that are refractory to direct assessment? How can we detect higher-order patterns of behavior?

In considering the cognitive economics of assessment paradigms, I concluded that *illusory correlation* is likely to affect medical and psychodynamic assessment based on clinical observations; *inability to assess covariation* is most likely to affect psychodynamic assessment, but may affect medical assessment that is based on clinical observations; the *representativeness heuristic* and *availability heuristic* affect all four paradigms; and the *confirmatory bias* affects paradigms that make strong causal assumptions, including the medical, psychodynamic, and behavioral paradigms. Each of the paradigms also has other limitations, such as the psychometric paradigm's lack of causal hypotheses; the psychodynamic paradigm's lack of testability; and the premature closure fostered by medical and behavioral convictions about the nature of behavior disorders.

3

OTHER APPROACHES TO ASSESSMENT

Beside the major paradigms for assessment of disordered behavior, there are several approaches that share certain characteristics of the major paradigms but have a more specialized focus. Some of these approaches are important adjuncts of the major paradigms and may contribute to the evolution of new and better assessment paradigms.

DEVELOPMENTAL ASSESSMENT

All approaches need to take account of the rapid changes that children continually undergo. Although the major paradigms have spawned different assessment techniques for individuals of different ages, they have not been explicitly designed to track developmental changes in maladaptive behavior. Efforts to tap development generally have assessed sequences of developmental achievements by scoring items according to the age at which a majority of children pass them, as first done by Binet and Simon (1905/1916). However, unlike the use of school performance as a validity criterion for the Binet scale, most developmental scales do not have a clear-cut external validity criterion. Instead, their developmental norms serve as an intrinsic criterion for determining how a child compares with his or her agemates. This is especially true during the infant and preschool periods, when developmental assessment is most common and when no external validity criterion has such general significance as school performance at later ages.

Some developmental tests, such as the Gesell Scales of Infant Development (Knobloch & Pasamanick, 1974), are based on a view of behavioral development as a form of embryological unfolding. According to this view, almost any major lag or deviation in patterning is considered pathological. Other developmental tests are designed to tap sequences and functions specified by more detailed theories of development. Uzgiris and Hunt's (1975) infant scales, for example, test cognitive development according to the stages hypothesized by Piaget. They use standardized versions of Piaget's experimental tasks, such as moving an object from one hiding place to another, to assess the development of the infant's concept of permanent objects.

Still other tests are constructed according to a normative-developmental approach, whereby items are selected and grouped mainly according to their statistical parameters in normative samples, such as the Bayley (1969) Scales of Infant Development and the Denver Developmental Screening Test (Frankenburg & Dodds, 1968). In an item typical of these measures, 6-month-old children are shown a mirror to determine whether they respond playfully.

Beside developmental tests, there are inventories for scoring parents' reports of their children's behavior in terms of developmentally normed scales. Examples are the Minnesota Child Development Inventory (Ireton & Thwing, 1974) and the Vineland Adaptive Behavior Scales (Sparrow, Cicchetti, & Balla, 1984), which are based on the Vineland Social Maturity Scale (Doll, 1965). These scales are composed of accomplishments that parents can observe in their child's everyday functioning, such as "feeds self without help" and "rides tricycle using pedals" from the Minnesota Child Development Inventory.

Developmental research has produced a vast array of procedures for testing hypothesized variables in specialized samples under controlled conditions (see Mussen, 1983). However, such research procedures are seldom sufficiently standardized for the clinical assessment of individual children. A major challenge for the developmental assessment of behavior disorders is to bridge the gap between basic developmental research and the practical exigencies of clinical assessment.

PSYCHOEDUCATIONAL ASSESSMENT

Intelligence tests laid the cornerstone for psychoeducational assessment. With the increasing systematization of public school curricula, however, children's educational progress has become a focus of assessment in its own right. Using a psychometric and normative-developmental format resembling intelligence tests, achievement tests are widely used to assess pupils' knowledge of standard curricular content. Whereas intelligence tests compare a child's cognitive ability with that of normal agemates, achievement tests compare a child's *knowledge* with that of children who are at a particular grade level in school. Intelligence tests generally predict achievement test scores fairly well, although achievement tests can reflect specific academic weaknesses not tapped by intelligence tests. When a child's achievement is much worse than predicted by an intelligence test, it may indicate either a lack of motivation or a learning disability that prevents the child from fully using his or her ability in school. Highly differentiated individual achievement tests, such as the Woodcock-Johnson Psychoeducational Battery (1977), yield profiles of academic abilities, achievement, and interests.

To illuminate suspected learning disabilities, psychoeducational assessment usually includes tests of perceptual integration. Koppitz (1977), for example, designed the Visual Aural Digit Span Test (VADS) to tap specific processes hypothesized to be deficient in learning disabled children. The VADS presents digits aurally (read aloud by the examiner) and visually (printed on cards). Children are asked to recall each type of input orally and by writing out the digits. The four combinations of input and output form four subtests: aural input-oral output; visual input-oral output; aural input-written output; and visual input-written output.

By testing immediate recall via the four subtests, the VADS aims to detect deficiencies in the integration of sights and sounds and in the sequencing and accuracy of recall. Children independently identified as learning disabled have been found to perform more poorly than normal children matched for age and IQ, indicating that the VADS taps learning problems not detected by the IQ (Koppitz, 1977).

Psychoeducational assessment focuses largely on achievement and abilities, but academic motivation is also an important variable. Adelman and Taylor (1983), for example, found that ratings of motivation among learning disabled students predicted absenteeism, behavior problems, and involvement in voluntary enrichment activities. This suggests that adequate motivation may be a prerequisite for overcoming academic and behavior problems identified through psychoeducational assessment.

Because most children with behavior disorders also have school problems, detailed psychoeducational assessment is often needed to identify specific patterns of ability, achievement, and dysfunction. As with other forms of assessment, however, there is a need for better validated techniques for determining the etiology, prognosis, and most appropriate management of children's school problems.

ASSESSMENT OF SKILLS AND COMPETENCIES

Many behavioral problems of childhood and adolescence involve a lack of skills and competencies. From a developmental perspective, deviance typically involves a failure to develop skills and competencies at the expected rate. Developmental measures should therefore gauge the degree to which children lag behind their agemates.

From a behavioral perspective, assessment should determine what new skills are needed to overcome existing problems and what changes are produced by interventions. Because it is hard to assess interpersonal skills nonreactively under naturalistic conditions, behavior modifiers often use analog situations such as role playing.

As research on role playing and other forms of skills assessment has accumulated, several problems have become evident. A basic problem arises in relating *molar skill categories,* such as assertiveness, to *molecular response components*, such as eye contact and voice volume (Bellack, 1979). Most clinical disorders and theory concern molar categories of deviance. Direct assessment, however, focuses on molecular response components that do not summate to the competencies that enable people to function effectively. Autistic children, for example, can be taught to increase their rate of eye contact and change their voice intonation, but this does not necessarily make them more skillful in social relationships. Furthermore, individuals are likely to differ greatly in the accuracy with which their real-life behavior is captured by the role playing situations used to test or train skills (McNamara & Blumer, 1982).

Competence as a Construct

As an alternative to the molecular approach of behavioral assessment, there have been efforts to define competence as a hypothetical construct. Waters and Sroufe (1983), for example, proposed social competence as a central developmental construct for integrating the study of individual differences across age levels, situations, and behavioral domains. Ford (1982) has hypothesized differentiated subsystems of personal functioning to account for social competence as a general characteristic. Each subsystem involves social cognitive variables that may predict social competence, which Ford defines as "the attainment of relevant social goals in specified social contexts, using appropriate means and resulting in positive developmental outcomes" (p. 324).

In an elaborate study Ford tested nine social cognitive predictors of social competence in ninth and twelfth graders. The predictors were self-report measures of variables such as empathy and goal-directedness. The social competence criterion measures included peer nominations and teacher ratings of social competence in six hypothetical situations. The peer nominations were obtained by having subjects name the three boys and three girls in their grade who would best be able to handle each of the six situations, such as the following:

> Everyone's complaining because this year all the teachers are assigning homework over Christmas vacation. Rather than just gripe about it, the students in your grade have gotten together and asked the teachers to listen to their side of the story. A group of teachers has agreed to talk with one of the students about their complaints at the next teachers' meeting. Who in your grade do you think could do the best job of getting across the students' point of view? (Ford, 1982, p. 339)

To test the ability of the nine social cognition variables to predict the peer and teacher judgments of social competence, Ford computed multiple regressions in one school and cross-validated them in another. In separate analyses of peer and teacher judgments for ninth and twelfth graders, Ford found that the nine social cognition variables collectively accounted for between 10 percent and 17 percent of the variance in the social competence measures.

Ford attempted to demonstrate the independence of his social cognition and social competence measures from general cognitive ability by factor analyzing the predictors, criterion measures, and two measures of ability (grade point average and group ability test scores). The largest factor was composed of four items: the two ability measures plus the peer nominations and teacher ratings for social competence. The fact that the social cognition predictors did not load on the same factor as the ability measures indicates their separateness from general ability. Yet the high loadings of the peer nominations and teacher ratings on the ability factor indicate that these measures of competence shared more variance with the two general ability measures than with the nine social cognition measures.

The importance of the ability measures in accounting for peer nominations and teacher ratings is also shown in the multiple regression equations: When the ability measures were added as predictors, the cross-validated variance in the second school ranged from 26 to 46 percent, as compared with 10 to 17 percent for the nine social cognition variables alone. The two ability measures thus appeared to contribute much more to the prediction of social competence than did the nine social cognition variables.

The difficulty of separating constructs of social competence from general cognitive ability was more directly illustrated in a study of adolescents' responses to hypothetical social situations such as the following:

> You're visiting your aunt in another part of town, and you don't know any of the guys your age there. You're walking along her street, and some guy is walking toward you. He is about your size. As he is about to pass you, he deliberately bumps into you, and you nearly lose your balance. What do you say or do now? (Freedman, Rosenthal, Donahoe, Schlundt, & McFall, 1978, p. 1450)

Rules derived from judgments by various criterion groups were used to score the competence indicated by the adolescents' responses. It was found that school leaders scored significantly higher than ordinary boys, who in turn scored significantly higher than delinquents. However, the scores correlated .70 with IQ. Like Ford's (1982) findings, this suggests that social competence assessed via judgments of functioning in hypothetical situations is significantly related to cognitive ability, as measured by intelligence tests.

Norm-Based Assessment of Competence

In addition to tests, role playing, and judgments of hypothetical situations, competence has been assessed by obtaining standardized parent and teacher reports of the quality and quantity of children's involvement in activities and interpersonal relationships (Achenbach

& Edelbrock, 1983). For example, parents are asked to list the recreational activities their child likes best, how proficient the child is in each one, and how often the child does it, compared to other children of the same age. Similar questions assess the child's involvement in organizations, jobs and chores, friendships, school, and relations with parents, siblings, and other people.

Parents' responses for normative samples of children grouped by age and sex provide standard scores that make it possible to compare parental reports for a particular child with those for typical agemates. Scores on scales designated as Activities, Social, and School discriminate significantly between children referred for mental health services and demographically similar nonreferred children. Although the social competence scores have significant (negative) correlations with behavior problem scores, most of the correlations are in the −.20s within referred and nonreferred samples (Achenbach & Edelbrock, 1983). This indicates that the social competence and behavior problem scores are not just mirror images of each other. The behavior problem scores generally discriminate more powerfully between referred and nonreferred children, but the addition of the social competence scores increases discriminative power and may help in tailoring interventions to existing strengths as well as deficits. Furthermore, the social competence scores correlate only .25 with IQ, indicating more independence from cognitive ability than most other social competence measures (McConaughy & Ritter, 1985). Considerable research is needed, however, to determine more precisely how the assessment of competence can contribute to services for children and adolescents.

ASSESSMENT OF SOCIAL COGNITION

In the study by Ford (1982) that was discussed earlier, social cognitive measures were tested as predictors of peer and teacher judgments of adolesents' competence in hypothetical situations. Social cognition has also become a major topic in its own right. One approach has been to apply cognitive developmental paradigms, such as Piaget's, to the study of children's thoughts about social phenomena (Flavell & Ross, 1981). It seems clear that inferences about emotions, motives, social interactions, other people's perspectives, and moral dilemmas depend on the development of cognitive operations like those required for understanding

TABLE 3.1
Interpersonal Cognitive Problem-Solving Skills

Skills	Examples
1. Generation of alternative solutions —thinking of a variety of categories of solutions to a problem.	A child wanting a toy from another child thinks of several means that might be tried.
2. Consideration of consequences of social acts—thinking beyond an act to what might happen if it's carried out.	An adolescent thinks of several possible positive and negative consequences of a contemplated act.
3. Means-ends thinking—mental representation of steps needed to solve a problem.	A child moving to a new neighborhood thinks about how to have a party that might attract new friends.
4. Social-causal thinking—understanding that feelings, actions, and problems are determined by prior events.	Failing to be selected for a school office won by a senior, a sophomore does not blame his or her personal shortcomings but understands that seniors have traditionally been chosen.
5. Sensitivity to problems—awareness of the varied potentials for social friction.	A child is able to specify a large variety of problems that arise between friends.
6. Dynamic orientation—the ability to look below the surface of human behavior.	A child understands that bullies may be trying to compensate for their own insecurity.

SOURCE: Spivack and Shure (1982).

physical phenomena. There is also evidence that the understanding of psychological defense mechanisms depends on the development of certain cognitive operations. The defense mechanism of projection, for example, does not seem to be understood without the cognitive abilities that Piaget called "formal operational," which are typically attained at about the age of 11 (Chandler, Paget, & Koch, 1978).

Interpersonal Cognitive Problem-Solving Skills

Beside the application of cognitive developmental paradigms to social phenomena, there have been efforts to assess and enhance interpersonal cognitive problem-solving skills. Spivack and Shure (1982), for example, have proposed that skills in reasoning about interpersonal

TABLE 3.2
Maladaptive Responses Due to Lack of Interpersonal
Cognitive Problem-Solving Skills

Maladaptive Responses	Examples
1. Not thinking—immediate surging ahead or withdrawing as a general trait or in response to situational stress.	A child responds impulsively to a frustrating experience with no effort at coping effectively.
2. Defensive thinking—neurotic conflicts interfere with the use of appropriate cognitive strategies.	A child interacts poorly with male teachers because of a fear of men in authority.
3. Preoccupation with possible alternative solutions—the generation of many alternatives is not matched by skill in choosing among them.	A child ruminates about many possible means to make friends but cannot carry any of them out.
4. Exaggeration of obstacles to solutions—rejection of all solutions because they appear doomed to fail.	An adolescent depressed about a lack of dates considers only the pitfalls of all possible solutions.

SOURCE: Spivack and Shure (1982).

situations are crucial for social adjustment. Table 3.1 lists some of the skills that Spivack and Shure have studied most extensively in children, and Table 3.2 lists maladaptive cognitive responses that may occur when these skills are lacking.

Spivack and Shure (1982) have assessed the hypothesized skills by means of tests and interviews that present hypothetical social situations. Children's responses are judged in terms of each skill, such as the generation of many alternative solutions, rather than by the actual solutions offered. Scores on several skills measures have correlated significantly with social adjustment and prosocial behavior in settings such as preschool and school classrooms. Training programs have also been shown to improve performance on the skills measures and, in some cases, subsequent social adjustment in a particular target context, such as school. This work has been widely acclaimed for its detailed training techniques usable by parents and teachers of children at several age levels. The techniques appear to have measurable effects on the test performance and behavior of general population samples and on self-control by at least some hyperactive and aggressive children (see Spivack & Shure, 1982).

Social Information Processing

Despite the appeal of the Spivack-Shure approach, Dodge (1983) has questioned the role of the general cognitive skills that they stress. He points out, for example, that aggressive children may not generate fewer problem solutions than nonaggressive children, but that their solutions are far more antagonistic. To link social cognitive assessment more closely to specific social behavior, Dodge divides social information processing into five steps:

Step 1: Encoding social cues in the environment.
Step 2: Mentally representing and interpreting the cues.
Step 3: Searching for possible behavioral responses.
Step 4: Deciding on an optimal response.
Step 5: Enacting the chosen response.

Whereas Spivack and Shure assess general skills that may collectively affect social cognition and behavior, Dodge traces the genesis of specific behaviors from an initial cue situation through the five-step sequence to a behavioral endproduct. He attempts to assess each step separately by holding each of the other steps constant. To assess the response decision skills of Step 4, for example, the preceding steps must be eliminated for all subjects. This can be done by giving subjects a choice of behavioral responses to a particular social cue and eliciting their response decision processes.

By studying different steps in the sequence, Dodge has found individual differences in information processing related to aggression. During the Step 1 encoding process, for example, nonaggressive boys were found to search for more cues prior to judging other people's behavior than did aggressive boys. During Step 2 aggressive boys were found to interpret ambiguous cues as indicating hostility more than did nonaggressive boys. Using multiple regression equations, Dodge has shown that measures of the five hypothesized information-processing steps collectively correlate with dependent variables, such as successful entry to a group, responding to provocations, and teachers' ratings of aggression. Cross-validation in new samples is needed, however, to determine the true magnitude of these relations.

To make clinical use of the hypothesized relations, Dodge has proposed the following plan for the assessment and treatment of aggression:

(1) To identify the domains of greatest difficulty, the clinician is to conduct detailed interviews with the child, parents, and teachers, and observe the child's social interactions.

(2) The clinician must then assess the child's processing of social information in the problematic situations.

(3) The clinician must design interventions for altering the child's processing of social information. Examples include didactic instruction, modeling, role playing, feedback, and reinforcement, but the clinician may also have to "design a social environment which is antithetical to the child's perception that others are hostile."

(4) The clinician must review the effectiveness of the intervention, including alterations of the child's social information processing, the child's behavior, and the referring agent's satisfaction that the child is no longer deviant.

Clinical applications of Dodge's information-processing model must thus face many of the problems faced by other approaches in obtaining reliable and valid pictures of the child's behavior in important real-life contexts. Assessing the social information processing of clinically referred children in real-life problem situations may be even harder than assessing their behavior, as is the design of special social environments, verifying changes in the child's information processing, and assuring the satisfaction of referring agents that the child is no longer deviant.

SOCIOMETRIC ASSESSMENT

Sociometric assessment obtains evaluations of individuals by their peers. For children and adolescents, school classes and activity groups are the usual settings for sociometric assessment. One method is to identify popular and unpopular members by asking each child to indicate which other children he or she would like to join in certain activities. Children who are not chosen by others are inferred to be the least popular. A related method aims to identify rejected children by having the participants indicate which peers they like least, as well as those they like most.

In a more differentiated method, each child chooses others for parts in a hypothetical class play (Bower, 1969). The parts are defined to reflect a greater variety of characteristics than popularity versus unpopularity or rejection. Another method is to specify characteristics of a hypothesized trait or condition, such as "Who often looks sad?" for assessing depression (Lefkowitz & Tesiny, 1980). Each participant names a peer who fits the description. When data are obtained individually from all members of a group, each child's score is the number of other children who nominated him or her for a particular characteristic.

Sociometric methods have been used in research on group dynamics, peer relations, and maladaptive behavior. Scores obtained for negative characteristics have been found to correlate with indices of psychopathology and to predict continuing problems over several years (Bower, 1969). Peer nominations for depressive characteristics have been found to be somewhat more stable over a period of six months than either teacher ratings or self-ratings for depression among elementary school students (Tesiny & Lefkowitz, 1982). Sociometric assessment has also been used in research on the specific behaviors of children who have trouble gaining acceptance and friendship (Coie & Kupersmidt, 1983; Dodge, 1983; Putallaz, 1983).

Sociometric research can contribute to the development of intervention techniques with children who lack appropriate social skills. Sociometric measures may also be useful for large-scale screening to identify children who are rejected. However, sociometric assessment of individual clinically referred children is limited by the need for cooperation from school systems, teachers, entire classes, and, often, parental permission for all the participating children. Furthermore, ethical issues are raised by children's discussion of their negative choices and by referred children's sensitivity to signs of rejection by peers (Hayvren & Hymel, 1984). In many cases, adequate judgments of unpopularity or rejection can be made by a teacher or trained observer who is already involved in the case without obtaining data directly from the child's peers.

ASSESSMENT OF FAMILY FUNCTIONING

Children's dependence on their families makes family functioning an important aspect of assessment. Some family therapists regard family problems as precursors of all childhood disorders (e.g., Ackerman, 1968). On the other hand, there is evidence that certain childhood disorders, such as infantile autism, contribute to problems in other family members (e.g., Schopler & Loftin, 1969). Whatever the direction of causation, there is abundant evidence of high rates of behavior disorders in the children of discordant families (Emery, 1982). Knowledge of the family and its special strengths and weaknesses is therefore always important in formulating intervention plans.

Family system therapists view the family rather than the individual as the primary focus of assessment. Because they believe that children's problems can only be understood as a facet of the family system, they hold that assessment must focus on characteristics of the family as a whole, such as the following:

(1) The family's strivings and values.
(2) The stability, maturity, and realism of the family.
(3) Regressive and disintegrative trends in the family.
(4) The quality and degree of successful adaptation (Ackerman & Behrens, 1974, p. 45).

Almost all clinical assessment of children includes information on the family history and constellation. Standardized interviews can yield good interparent agreement and interrater reliability for parents' reports of some aspects of family functioning (Brown & Rutter, 1966). To provide a more comprehensive picture, Moos and Moos (1981) have developed the Family Environment Scale, which consists of true/false items such as "We fight a lot in our family" and "Friends often come over for dinner or to visit." The items are scored on a profile of ten scales, including Cohesion, Conflict, Achievement, and Independence. By having adolescents and parents fill out the scale to describe current family conditions and their preferred family conditions, the profiles reflecting each member's perceptions and preferences can be compared to identify areas of agreement and disagreement. The results can be shared with the family members as a way of clarifying family dynamics and setting treatment goals (e.g., Moos & Fuhr, 1982).

The direct assessment of family functioning advocated by family therapists is much more complex. In an extensive study, for example, families were videotaped under standardized conditions as they dealt with tasks designed to highlight positive and negative family characteristics (Lewis, Beavers, Gossett, & Phillips, 1976). One task presented a recorded vignette in which a family member is in danger of dying. After the vignette ended on an ambiguous note, the family was asked to make up an ending to the story. Other tasks required the family to plan something together and to discuss their family's strengths and weaknesses.

Trained observers were able to achieve adequate reliability in ratings of family health versus pathology, overall mood, invasiveness (speaking for one another), and permeability (receptiveness to one another's statements). The ratings also discriminated between families with and without a disturbed adolescent and between families judged to be functioning optimally versus those functioning only adequately. Family strengths were at least as important as family problems in determining the judged level of functioning.

This study showed that family systems concepts can be translated into reliable and discriminating assessment procedures. However, the family measures did not correlate well with assessment of psychopathology in the family members as individuals. Furthermore, there is evidence that observers and observation settings affect family interactions (Hetherington & Martin, 1979) and that evaluation of family members together is followed by more dropouts from therapy than is individual evaluation (Shapiro & Budman, 1973). Because procedures like those of Lewis et al. (1976) are costly and do not yield a clear basis for prediction or intervention, more work is needed to adapt direct family assessment to the assessment of children and adolescents.

ECOLOGICAL ASSESSMENT

Beside techniques for assessing the behavior of children and their families, efforts have been made to assess ecological factors in maladaptive behavior. Like behavioral assessment, ecological assessment assumes that behavior is shaped by the natural environment. The focus of assessment, however, is more on the environment itself than on the child's behavior. Instead of viewing a child as hyperactive, for example, an ecological approach examines the conditions and expectations of the environment, such as the school classroom, where the child's behavior is judged deviant.

Teacher Expectations

There have been few attempts to develop standardized ecological assessment procedures for children's behavior disorders per se. The Social Behavioral Survival (SBS) Inventory of Teacher Social Behavior

Standards and Expectations, however, is designed to assess the types of positive child behavior that a teacher considers essential in the classroom and the types of negative behavior that the teacher considers unacceptable (Walker & Rankin, 1983). An example of a positive behavior item is "Child cooperates with peers in group activities or situations." A negative item is "Child ignores teacher warnings or reprimands."

The SBS Inventory indicates a teacher's readiness to accept handicapped children and the teacher's specific needs for help with them. Walker and Rankin found large differences between the responses of some individual teachers; but teacher trainees, regular class teachers, and special education teachers obtained similar group averages. This suggests that experience and training did not greatly alter teachers' general standards and expectations for classroom conduct. Although the SBS Inventory was designed mainly to assess the prospects for placement of handicapped children in mainstream classes, a similar approach may have potential for assessing teacher expectations about behavior problems.

Environmental Conditions

Another ecological approach involves the assessment of general environmental conditions. The Caldwell Home Observation for Measurement of the Environment (HOME) Inventory, for example, is designed to identify homes that are likely to impede or foster cognitive development (Caldwell & Bradley, 1979). A version for children under 3 years old includes scales for emotional and verbal responsivity of mother; avoidance of restriction and punishment; organization of the environment; appropriate play materials; maternal involvement with child; and variety in daily stimulation. A home visitor makes yes/no judgments of each item, such as "Child has push or pull toy" and "Mother reads stories at least three times weekly." A version of the HOME Inventory for ages 3 to 6 includes variants of some of the infant scales, plus scales for pride, attention, and warmth; stimulation of academic behavior; and modeling of social maturity. Although norms are not provided, there is evidence that scores significantly predict preschool mental development within particular groups of at-risk children, such as low birthweight infants (Siegel, 1982).

In the section on family functioning, we discussed the Family Environment Scale (Moos & Moos, 1981). Although it is used by family therapists to assess family systems, it is an extension of Moos's efforts to assess the social ecology of institutional environments, such as prisons, work places, mental hospitals, and schools. The profiles derived from the Family Environment Scale can therefore be viewed as reflecting the social ecology of the home, at least as reported by parents. Cluster analyses of the profiles have yielded six ecological patterns designated as Expression-Oriented; Achievement-Oriented; Moral/Religious-Oriented; and Conflict-Oriented (Moos & Moos, 1976). Scales for listing stressful life events, such as the death of a family member, have also been used for research on precipitants of psychopathology, mainly in adults (e.g., Harder, Strauss, Kokes, Ritzler, & Gift, 1980).

CONTRIBUTIONS AND LIMITATIONS

Each of the assessment approaches considered in this chapter has a more specialized focus than the major paradigms considered in Chapter 2. Developmental approaches apply psychometric principles to the assessment of developmental sequences. Developmental scales, such as the Bayley (1969) and Gesell Scales (Knobloch & Pasamanick, 1974), are cornerstones of the clinical assessment of infants and young children, but most research procedures for testing developmental hypotheses are quite remote from clinical assessment of behavior disorders. In Chapter 5 we will consider implications of developmental research for the assessment and taxonomy of behavior disorders.

Psychoeducational assessment is largely an application of the psychometric paradigm to an area that should be closely allied with the assessment of behavior disorders, as children who have behavior disorders often have problems in school. Differentiated assessment of school achievement and ability can potentially guide the educational aspects of interventions for children with behavior disorders. Effective psychoeducational assessment requires a better taxonomy of school-related disorders, however, and better integration with assessment of children's behavior under various school-related conditions.

The five remaining areas that we considered—skills and competencies, social cognition, sociometric, family functioning, and ecological—focus on limited sets of variables hypothesized to be of great importance for behavioral adaptation. Each of them has engendered abundant theory and a few measures that may shed light on adaptive processes.

Their relatively limited focus and the paucity of well-validated, practical procedures for clinical assessment, however, make them unlikely to become general assessment paradigms in the near future. Instead, their immediate value may be in calling attention to important perspectives neglected by the four major paradigms. These perspectives may aid in efforts to overcome the biases and limitations of the prevailing paradigms.

SUMMARY

Specialized assessment approaches deserve consideration for their potential contributions to more comprehensive assessment. Developmental sequences may be especially important in understanding child and adolescent psychopathology, but standardized developmental assessment has been used mainly with infants and preschoolers. Most of the standardized assessment procedures are modeled on the normative-developmental approach pioneered in the Binet intelligence scale, although some are based on developmental theories such as Piaget's. Few of the numerous procedures devised for developmental research have been refined sufficiently for clinical assessment of individual children.

Psychoeducational assessment includes numerous procedures for appraising ability, achievement, and other aspects of school functioning. Many of the procedures are standardized according to psychometric principles and can be used to assess the academic functioning of children with behavior disorders. A major challenge is to integrate assessment of hypothesized academic impediments, such as learning disabilities, with assessment of the behavioral problems that often accompany them.

Social competence and social cognition have become popular topics of research and theory from several different perspectives. A major challenge is to determine how social aspects of competence and cognition relate to and differ from general cognitive ability. A second challenge is to find effective ways to relate molecular aspects of competence and cognition to more molar constructs.

Sociometric assessment has been used mainly in research on evaluations of children by their peers. This research has shown that scores obtained from groups of peers are significantly associated with other indices of social functioning. Logistical and ethical problems, however, make it impractical to use current sociometric techniques for routine clinical assessment of individual children.

Assessment of family functioning originated with family systems theory and therapy. Much of the literature on family assessment is based on therapists' clinical observations, but structured observations of families interacting under controlled conditions have shown that ratings can reliably distinguish between better and worse functioning families. Although this has supported certain family systems concepts, the controlled observation conditions are impractical for routine clinical assessment. Taking an ecological approach, Moos has developed an inventory of family characteristics that yields a typology of family patterns. Because the inventory can be filled out by family members, it may be a useful adjunct to clinical assessment, if the patterns are found to have important correlates.

Ecological assessment focuses on environmental characteristics and expectations as important variables in their own right. Efforts pertaining to children's behavior include assessment of teachers' expectations, home environments, and family characteristics. Further development of these approaches can potentially provide an important complement to assessment of children themselves.

4

TAXONOMIC PARADIGMS

As we saw in Chapters 2 and 3, assumptions about the nature of deviance affect the information that is sought, the mental processing of the information, and the application of previous knowledge to each case. The variety of assessment techniques attests to the multitude of potentially important distinguishing features. Information-processing biases, however, limit the effectiveness with which we utilize these distinguishing features. To sharpen the detection of distinguishing features, standardized assessment procedures compare people with one another in a consistent fashion. This is an important step in determining the ways in which one individual resembles and differs from others, but not all individual differences are of equal importance. Both the choice of what to assess and the interpretation of what is found are guided by our concepts of the target disorders.

Whether we favor medical, psychodynamic, behavioral, or family dynamic concepts, we necessarily abstract a few features from the many that distinguish individuals from one another. When we selectively abstract features to define disorders, we are engaging in a process of *taxonomy*. Whether taxonomy is implicit or explicit, it shapes our choice of assessment procedures, our interpretation of assessment data, and our conclusions. Conversely, a taxonomy requires reliable and valid assessment procedures for discriminating between individuals according to the defining criteria of the taxa.

As two facets of what should be a continuous process, assessment and taxonomy raise related problems of cognitive economics. In this chapter we consider ways in which taxonomic paradigms deal with these problems.

THE KRAEPELINIAN TAXONOMIC PARADIGM

As discussed in Chapter 2, nineteenth-century medicine assumed that mental disorders were brain diseases (Griesinger, 1845), each of which caused a distinctive syndrome of signs and symptoms. It was expected that clinical descriptions of syndromes would lead to the discovery of an organic cause for each disorder. Mental disorders were thus expected to join physical disorders in a general medical taxonomy or *nosology* (classification of diseases). An additional source of interest in clinical description was the growth of more humane institutional care for the mentally disturbed. Reliable descriptions of disorders were needed to facilitate separation of patients requiring different types of care, such as the violent versus the depressed and suicidal.

The prototype for the clinical description of mental disorders was paresis, which we discussed in Chapter 2. Once the syndrome of paresis was reliably identified, research could focus on individuals who were all assumed to suffer from the same underlying organic abnormality. Indeed, autopsies of people who died of paresis revealed brain inflammations that were eventually traced to syphilis. Success in isolating first the syndrome of paresis and then its underlying organic cause helped to establish the nosological model for mental disorders. The identification of organic syndromes among the mentally retarded also supported the nosological model. In 1866, for example, *Down syndrome* was delineated by Langdon Down, an Englishman who thought the "mongoloid" facial features were an evolutionary throwback to the "mongol race." In this case, however, it took nearly a hundred years to discover that an extra chromosome was responsible (Lejeune, Gautier, & Turpin, 1963).

Although clinical descriptions could pinpoint clearcut organic abnormalities, the many cases that lacked such abnormalities spawned conflicting descriptions. Where organic abnormalities were not evident, an overarching set of principles was needed to discriminate between syndromes. Amid a variety of efforts to construct a general taxonomy, the most influential was published in 1883 by Emil Kraepelin and continually revised until his death in 1926.

True to the nineteenth-century psychiatric ideal, Kraepelin wrote in 1881 that "the most important achievement which the advance of scientific research has brought to psychiatry in our century is the firm foundation of the notion of the somatic basis of mental disorders" (quoted by Kahn, 1959, p. 7). In the first edition of his taxonomy, Kraepelin (1883) relied on descriptive features to distinguish between disorders of unknown etiology. During the 1890s, however, he added course and prognosis as criteria for certain disorders. These criteria became especially important by 1896, when he distinguished between manic-depressive psychoses and dementia praecox (renamed "schizophrenia" by Bleuler in 1911), largely on the basis of differential prognosis. People who recovered were judged to be manic-depressive, whereas those who deteriorated were judged to have dementia praecox.

Beside using outcome data, Kraepelin also adapted then-current psychological methods to the study of his patients' mental processes. By 1915 he included a category of "psychogenic" disorders, including functional neuroses and traumatic psychoses. He placed personality disorders in a separate category, bordering between illness and common eccentricity.

Diagnostic and Statistical Manual of Mental Disorders (DSM)

The main categories of Kraepelin's system have continued to shape the American Psychiatric Association's (APA) *Diagnostic and Statistical Manual of Mental Disorders (DSM)*. However, successive editions of the *DSM* have taken different approaches to childhood disorders. In *DSM*-I (APA, 1952), most disorders were designated as "reactions," embodying Adolf Meyer's concept of mental disorders as reactions by the whole person or "psychobiologic unit" to stress (Lief, 1948). Disorders of unknown etiology were defined with a mixture of narrative description and psychodynamic inference. Reflecting the long neglect of children in psychiatric taxonomy, only two categories were provided for childhood disorders. These were "Schizophrenic Reaction, Childhood, Type" and "Adjustment Reaction of Infancy, Childhood, or Adolescence." Although adult diagnostic categories could also be applied to children, most children seen for mental health services either were diagnosed as having adjustment reactions or received no diagnosis (Achenbach, 1966; Rosen, Bahn, & Kramer, 1964).

DSM-II (APA, 1968) departed from *DSM*-I mainly in dispensing with Adolf Meyer's term "reaction" for adult disorders, but it also added the following behavior disorders of childhood and adolescence, which were designated as "reactions": "Hyperkinetic Reaction"; "Withdrawing Reaction"; "Overanxious Reaction"; "Runaway Reaction"; "Unsocialized Aggressive Reaction"; and "Group Delinquent Reaction." Although these categories were suggested by empirical research (e.g., Jenkins & Boyer, 1968), they were defined in terms of narrative description and inference like the other categories of *DSM*-I and *DSM*-II.

"Adjustment Reaction" remained the most commonly used category for childhood disorders (American Academy of Child Psychiatry, 1983).

DSM-III (APA, 1980) added more disorders of infancy, childhood, and adolescence, and changed the way disorders were specified. One major change was to provide five dimensions or axes. Axis I (clinical syndromes) and Axis II (personality and developmental disorders) correspond to traditional psychiatric taxonomies. The other three axes were designed to list physical illness (Axis III) and to provide ratings of psychosocial stress (Axis IV) and the person's highest level of adaptive functioning during the previous year (Axis V). These three axes supplement but do not directly affect the Kraepelinian taxonomy of Axes I and II.

For the Axis I and II disorders, *DSM*-III departed from previous editions by providing explicit criteria for each category. In most childhood categories, four types of criteria were provided:

(1) A list of behaviors from which a specified number must be present in order to meet criterion.
(2) A minimum period during which the behaviors specified in 1 must be present (e.g., two weeks).
(3) An age criterion (e.g., age at least 2½ before the category can be used).
(4) Criteria for excluding a particular diagnosis if the disorder is "due to" certain other disorders.

As an example, the *DSM*-III criteria for Attention Deficit Disorder with Hyperactivity (ADD+H) require the presence of at least three out of a list of five behavioral signs of inattention, such as "often fails to finish things he or she starts"; three out of a list of six signs of impulsivity, such as "often acts before thinking"; and two out of a list of five signs of hyperactivity, such as "runs about or climbs on things excessively." The duration criterion requires that the disorder be present for at least six months. The age criterion requires onset before the age of 7. The exclusionary criterion states that the disorder must not be "due to Schizophrenia, Affective Disorder, or Severe or Profound Mental Retardation." A draft revision of *DSM*-III (*DSM*-III-R) retains these general principles, but reduces the subtyping of childhood disorders, the subgrouping of descriptive criteria within disorders, and the number of exclusionary criteria.

Group for the Advancement of Psychiatry (GAP)

Dissatisfied with the neglect of children in *DSM*-I, the Group for the Advancement of Psychiatry (GAP, 1966) formulated a taxonomy of child and adolescent disorders, as outlined in Table 4.1. The general approach resembled *DSM*-I and *DSM* II in that mixtures of narrative descriptions and inferences were negotiated by committees of psychiatrists. The GAP proposed far more categories of childhood disorders, however, and sought to incorporate developmental considerations, largely from psychodynamic theory. The proposed taxonomy also included a category of healthy responses to developmental crises, such as the separation anxiety 6-month-old babies show whenever their mothers leave and identity crises in adolescents.

Many of the GAP categories do not have clear counterparts in the *DSM*, and vice versa. Hyperactive behavior, for example, is subject to varying interpretations in the GAP taxonomy, as follows:

> *Deviations in motor development* include long-continued deviations in psychomotor functions and activity levels (hyperactivity, hypoactivity), and deviations in coordination, handedness, and other predominantly motoric capacities in which brain damage or other factors do not appear to be involved. Some hyperkinetic children without brain damage would be considered in this category; other deviations, where anxiety produced the hyperactivity, would be classified under reactive disorders or under appropriate total personality categories, with the hyperactivity listed as a symptom. (GAP, 1966, pp. 226-227)

As with most GAP categories, there are no explicit criteria for determining whether a child qualifies for the "Deviations in Motor Development" category or the other categories mentioned, such as reactive disorders or personality disorders.

World Health Organization (WHO)

A World Health Organization (WHO) seminar proposed a multiaxial taxonomy for children's disorders (Rutter, Shaffer, & Shepherd, 1975). Like the *DSM* and GAP committees, the WHO group derived

TABLE 4.1
Outline of GAP (1966) Categories

I.   Healthy Responses
     A. Developmental crisis
     B. Situational crisis
     C. Other responses

II. Reactive Disorders

III. Developmental Deviations
     A. Deviations in maturational
        patterns
     B. Deviations in specific dimensions
        of development (Motor, sensory,
        speech, cognitive, social,
        psychosexual, affective, or
        integrative)

IV. Psychoneurotic Disorders
     A. Anxiety
     B. Phobic
     C. Conversion
     D. Dissociative
     E. Obsessive-compulsive
     F. Depressive
     G. Other

V.   Personality Disorders
     A. Compulsive
     B. Hysterical
     C. Anxious
     D. Overly dependent
     E. Oppositional
     F. Overly inhibited
     G. Overly independent
     H. Isolated
     I. Mistrustful
     J. Tension-discharge disorders
        1. Impulse-ridden
        2. Neurotic personality
     K. Sociosyntonic
     L. Sexual deviation
     M. Other

VI. Psychotic Disorders
     A. Psychoses of infancy and early
        childhood
        1. Early infantile autism
        2. Interactional psychotic disorder
        3. Other
     B. Psychoses of later childhood
        1. Schizophreniform psychotic
           disorder
        2. Other
     C. Psychoses of adolescence
        1. Acute confusional state
        2. Schizophrenic disorder, adult
           type
        3. Other

VII. Psychophysiologic Disorders
     (Specific sites are listed)

VIII. Brain Syndromes
      (Acute, chronic)

IX. Mental Retardation

X.   Other Disorders

definitions from their own clinical concepts of disorders. However, the axes proposed by the WHO seminar differ from those of the *DSM*. The four WHO axes are "psychiatric syndromes"; "intellectual level"; "biological factors"; and "psychosocial influences." The latter two resemble Axes III and IV of the *DSM*, although they are intended for all relevant biological, psychological, and social factors. The ninth edition of the *International Classification of Disease (ICD-9*; WHO, 1978) added a fifth axis for developmental lags.

Placing intellectual level on a separate axis avoids problems arising from *DSM*-III's inclusion of mental retardation as an Axis I psychiatric syndrome. For example, *DSM*-III excluded certain diagnoses, such as ADD, if "due to" mental retardation. This implies that mental retardation is a cause of ADD. Yet because some retarded children would not otherwise meet the criteria for ADD, *DSM*-III made it impossible to distinguish between those who do and those who do not have ADD problems. Furthermore, clinicians making an Axis I diagnosis of mental retardation might assume that this completes their Axis I work, causing them to omit other Axis I diagnoses that may be warranted (Rutter & Shaffer, 1980).

Diagnosis and Classification

"To diagnose" literally means "to distinguish" or "to know apart" (from Greek *dia* = apart, *gignoskein* = to know). Confusion arises, however, because the term "diagnosis" has acquired two different meanings. In one meaning, diagnosis is defined by a leading psychiatric diagnostician as "the medical term for classification" (Guzé, 1978, p. 53). Kraepelinian categories are often called "diagnoses," and the process of assigning cases to the categories is said to involve a diagnostic judgment. A diagnosis in this sense is called a *formal diagnosis*. It is the sense in which the *DSM*'s Axis I and Axis II categories are "diagnoses." When we decide, for example, that a girl meets the *DSM* criteria for conduct disorder, we are making a formal diagnosis.

The second meaning of diagnosis is broader. It is defined as an "investigation or analysis of the cause or nature of a condition, situation, or problem," and "a statement or conclusion concerning the nature or cause of some phenomenon" (Woolf, 1977, p. 313). When the term "diagnosis" is used in its broad sense, it refers to *diagnostic work-ups* and *diagnostic formulations*—the process of gathering information needed to understand an individual's problems and the formulation of a conclusion in a comprehensive fashion. Thus, although the girl's formal diagnosis is Conduct Disorder, the diagnostic work-up involves information and judgments about the girl's developmental history, possible etiology, strengths, vulnerabilities, treatment options, and prognosis. The diagnostic work-up is almost synonymous with "assessment," a term often preferred for its greater breadth than the disease-oriented term "diagnosis." A diagnostic formulation should weave all the findings of the diagnostic work-up into a comprehensive idiographic picture of the individual. A formal diagnosis, by contrast, abstracts attributes that link the individual to similar individuals presumed to have the same disorder.

The diagnosis of a disorder in terms of a *DSM* category is a formal diagnosis—a diagnosis in the sense of "classification" (Guzé, 1978). It does not mean that the disorder is understood more fully than if it were classified in terms of a taxonomy that is not called a "diagnostic system." Instead, the value of a taxonomy depends on such factors as its reliability, validity, contribution to clear communication, and ability to mark differences in cause, need for particular interventions, and prognosis.

Current Status of the Kraepelinian Paradigm

Taxonomies are intended to help us deal with complex phenomena by abstracting certain attributes as a basis for grouping individuals or disorders. Each category of a taxonomy represents a hypothetical construct defined by attributes that are singled out from all the other attributes that characterize individuals. Individuals and disorders can be classified in multiple ways, depending on the attributes and principles chosen as a basis for classification. When mental disorders came under the purview of nineteenth-century medicine, it was assumed that clinical descriptions would yield classes of disorders that would each be found to have a specific organic cause. After some initial success in identifying syndromes marked by organic signs and symptoms, a general system was needed to discriminate between disorders of unknown etiology that lacked obvious organic features. Kraepelin's system was originally intended as a descriptive nosology, but later revisions went far beyond the description of signs and symptoms.

Instead of deriving disorders from empirical data, current versions of Kraepelinian taxonomy—such as the *DSM*, GAP, WHO, and *ICD*-9—define disorders via debate and negotiation. As employed in *DSM*-III, this procedure was described as starting

with a clinical concept for which there is some degree of face validity. Face validity is the extent to which the description of a particular category seems on the face of it to describe accurately the characteristic features of persons with a particular disorder. It is the result of clinicians agreeing on the identification of a particular syndrome or pattern of clinical features as a mental disorder. Initial criteria are generally developed by asking the clinicians to describe what they consider to be the most characteristic features of the disorder. (Spitzer & Cantwell, 1980, p. 369)

Such taxonomies thus translate clinical concepts (i.e., hypothetical constructs) into categorical criteria. Certain constructs, such as adult schizophrenia and manic-depressive conditions, have a long history of research and theory. Several sets of research diagnostic criteria (RDC) have been developed to improve the reliability and validity with which adult disorders are classified in terms of these constructs. Although different sets of RDC disagree in classifying cases (see Overall & Hollister, 1979), experience gained with the RDC contributed to the formulation of *DSM*-III criteria for adult disorders. Yet neither the RDC nor the *DSM*-III provide "operational" criteria in terms of standardized assessment operations. The *DSM*-III childhood disorders have an especially weak empirical basis, because few had been researched and there were no RDC for any of them.

Reliability

In view of the meager empirical basis for the childhood disorders, how should we evaluate contemporary Kraepelinian taxonomies? A basic consideration is the reliability with which a taxonomy's categories are used. This has two main facets: *Interjudge reliability* concerns agreement between different users in their assignment of cases to the taxonomy's categories; *test-retest reliability* concerns the agreement between a particular user's assignment of the same cases to the taxonomy's categories on two occasions. Test-retest reliability may be reduced by changes in characteristics of the cases as well as inconsistencies in the judge making the assignments. As yet, there has been little research on the test-retest reliability of Kraepelinian taxonomies of childhood disorders. There are, however, several studies of the interjudge reliability of the WHO, *ICD*-9, GAP, and *DSM*-III taxonomies.

Judgments from Case Histories

In the one study of the WHO, both studies of the *ICD*-9 and GAP, and two of the five *DSM*-III studies, participants made their judgments from written case histories. This method ensures that each judge receives exactly the same data on the cases, judges do not influence one another, and the data are concretely documented. It is vulnerable, however, to biases in what is presented, which can either inflate agreement by highlighting data conforming to taxonomic criteria or reduce agreement by omitting data obtainable through direct involvement with a case. (A study of adult *DSM*-III diagnoses, for example, showed generally higher agreement for live interviews than for case materials; Hyler, Williams, & Spitzer, 1982.)

Most of the studies reported reliability in terms of the percentage of agreement between judges, which may be inflated by chance agreements. To take an extreme example, if two judges use a particular category for all cases or if they use a category for no cases, their agreement will be 100 percent. This impressive figure is misleading, because neither judge made any discriminations between cases.

Despite possible inflation by chance agreements, the overall rate of agreement was only 40% and 59% for broad categories such as personality versus psychotic disorders in the two GAP studies (Beitchman, Dielman, Landis, Benson, & Kemp, 1978; Freeman, 1971); 54% for *DSM*-III Axis I diagnoses (Mattison, Cantwell, Russell, & Will, 1979); 62% for the *ICD*-9 (Remschmidt, 1985); and 67% for the WHO (Rutter et al., 1975). Specific categories showed considerably less agreement in the three studies that analyzed them separately (Beitchman et al., 1978; Freeman, 1971; Remschmidt, 1985). In studies using the statistic kappa to correct for chance agreement, an overall kappa of .23 was obtained for *DSM*-III Axis I categories, .26 for Axis II categories, and .38 for *ICD*-9 (Gould, Shaffer, & Rutter, 1985; Mezzich & Mezzich, 1979). A kappa of .00, indicates chance agreement, whereas a kappa of 1.00 indicates perfect agreement, corrected for chance. Kappas below .60 generally indicate unacceptably poor reliability (Hartmann, 1977).

DSM-III Field Trials

The *DSM*-III (APA, 1980) reported kappas for agreement between pairs of clinicians participating in field trials of *DSM*-III. The clinicians voluntarily submitted data according to general instructions but, as Rutter and Shaffer (1980) point out, selective biases could affect the results obtained. Some clients were jointly interviewed by two clinicians, for example, whereas others were seen separately by the clinicians. The choice of cases, amount of communication between paired clinicians, and selectivity in submitting the data all could affect the reliability estimates. Although the specific figures should therefore not be taken literally, they do suggest three conclusions:

First, despite counting discrepant judgments as agreements if they fell within very broad categories, the reliability was not good. For the final version of Axis I, the overall kappa for child and adolescent disorders was .52. For Axis II the kappa was .55, even though all 18 specific disorders were grouped into two categories, developmental disorders and personality disorders.

Second, reliability was better for adults than children on all four axes that were assessed. The overall kappas were .72 for adults versus .52 for children on Axis I; .64 versus .55 on Axis II; intraclass correlations were .66 versus .59 on Axis IV (severity of psychosocial stressors); and .80 versus .52 on Axis V (highest level of attained functioning).

Third, reliability for children and adolescents declined from an early draft to the final draft used in the field trials. On Axis I, kappa declined from .68 to .52; on Axis II from .66 to .55; on Axis IV the correlation declined from .75 to .59; and on Axis V from .77 to .52. In contrast to these declines, the reliability for adults improved on the same four axes.

Judgments of Inpatients

Although some inpatients may have been included in the other reliability studies, two studies focused exclusively on inpatients. In one study (Strober, Green, & Carlson, 1981) two clinicians jointly interviewed inpatient adolescents (ages 12-17) and a family member, using the highly structured Schedule for Affective Disorders and Schizophrenia (SADS) supplemented by questions about development, physical health, school, and such. The clinicians reviewed all other available information, including school records, referral notes, and nursing observations. The second study based judgments on oral case presentations (Werry, Methven, Fitzpatrick, & Dixon, 1983). The number of judges ranged from two to four, depending on several factors, but "[mostly] the punctiliousness of the raters in completing their sheets" (p. 343). Strober et al. used an early draft of *DSM*-III for all cases, whereas Werry et al. used the early draft for most of their cases.

Both studies reported kappas for agreements occurring within broad categories like those assessed in the *DSM* field trials (e.g., all conduct disorders grouped together; all "other disorders" grouped together). The overall kappas of .74 (Strober) and .71 (Werry) were slightly higher than the kappa of .68 obtained with the early draft of the *DSM* used in the first field trial and considerably higher than the kappa of .52 obtained with the later draft of *DSM* used in the last field trial.

Perhaps the changes that improved reliabilities for adult disorders from the early to the later draft of *DSM*-III adversely affected the reliabilities for child and adolescent disorders. Or perhaps the quality of data, severity of the disorders characterizing inpatients, or the specific research procedures account for the higher reliabilities obtained by Strober and Werry. In the Strober study, for example, the involvement of both judges in the interviews and in the Werry study the "punctiliousness of the raters" who actually submitted diagnoses could have increased interjudge agreement. Even with the better overall agreement for broad categories, however, many specific categories and some of the broad categories still yielded extremely low kappas. Furthermore, as in the case history studies, judges were exposed to identical data. This would have protected their judgments from variations in available data and unreliability in the data themselves, both of which may reduce agreement under typical clinical conditions.

Test-Retest Reliability

In the one study of test-retest reliability of the judges themselves, Freeman (1971) found 72% agreement (uncorrected for chance) between GAP diagnoses made by psychiatrists from the same case histories at a three-month interval. Because there were no changes in the information about each case, this suggests that inconsistencies in the judges themselves limit the reliability of the GAP system and perhaps the others as well.

Validity

A taxonomy cannot be validly applied unless it is reliable, but reliability does not guarantee validity. In the passage quoted earlier from Spitzer and Cantwell (1980), "face validity" refers to a judgment by the authors of a category that their description of the category accurately represents the construct they have in mind. However, better evidence of validity is needed than the authors' satisfaction with their descriptions. Because we lack preexisting validity criteria to tell us what disorders truly exist, a taxonomy must be validated largely in terms of its relation to other criteria that are themselves recognized as imperfect. Both the taxonomy and the external criteria may need to be progressively revised in order to improve the taxonomy. Although current Kraepelinian taxonomies are not defined via empirical assessment procedures, empirical data should guide revisions of taxonomies just as they should guide revisions of assessment procedures.

As an example of relevant data, clinical interviews designed to operationalize diagnoses showed that 79% of children seen in a mental health clinic met the *DSM*-III criteria for Oppositional Disorder (Costello, Edelbrock, Dulcan, Kalas, & Kloric, 1984), specified as follows (APA, 1980, p. 65):

A pattern, for at least six months, of disobedient, negativistic, and provocative opposition to authority figures, as manifested by at least two of the following symptoms:

(1) violations of minor rules
(2) temper tantrums
(3) argumentativeness
(4) provocative behavior
(5) stubbornness

In the Costello et al. (1984) study, many children who met the criteria for Oppositional Disorder also met the criteria for Attention Deficit Disorder and one or more Conduct Disorders. This suggests that (1) Oppositional Disorder was defined by problem behaviors too common to discriminate meaningfully among children; (2) the criteria for Oppositional, Attention Deficit, and Conduct Disorders overlapped excessively. The same study revealed many logical contradictions and inconsistencies in the *DSM* criteria for excluding particular disorders as "due to" other disorders. Other research findings may likewise have implications for questions of validity. If classification according to particular categories were shown to be associated with different etiologies or differential responsiveness to particular treatments, for example, this would support the construct validity of those categories.

Key Questions

The original model for Kraepelinian taxonomy was nineteenth-century medical nosology, which assumed a physical cause for every syndrome. This model encouraged clinical descriptions that successfully identified syndromes featuring clearcut organic abnormalities and/or floridly deviant thoughts and behavior, such as found in adult paresis, schizophrenia, and manic-depressive conditions. The application of Kraepelinian taxonomy to childhood behavior disorders raises the following questions:

(1) How appropriate is the Kraepelinian model for problem behaviors that many children show at some time to some degree without evidence of physical pathology?
(2) How can current Kraepelinian approaches make better use of empirical data to identify and operationally define childhood disorders?
(3) All taxonomic paradigms require selective abstraction of attributes. What are the advantages and disadvantages of categorical clinical concepts for doing this, as compared to other approaches?

THE PSYCHODYNAMIC TAXONOMIC PARADIGM

As discussed in Chapter 2, psychodynamic theory originated in response to nineteenth-century medicine's failure to explain hysterical symptoms. In seeking explanations, Freud hypothesized that hysterical, obsessional, and phobic neuroses all involved the ego's efforts to repress unacceptable thoughts. Owing to preexisting differences between their personalities, however, hysterics, obsessionals, and phobics used repression in different ways. In hysterics the unacceptable thought and affect were both forced out of consciousness, but the affect was converted to somatic excitation that disturbed bodily functions. Obsessionals and phobics, by contrast, repressed the connection between the unacceptable thought and its affect. Both the thought and affect remained conscious, but the thought was shorn of affect, which then triggered other thoughts, obsessions, or irrational phobias. As Freud's theory of childhood sexuality evolved, he hypothesized that different types of neurosis stemmed from different types of childhood sexual experience.

In 1926, Freud drastically revised his theory of neurosis. Instead of viewing neurotic anxiety as a by-product of repression, he now saw it as a response to cues associated with traumatic experiences of childhood. This *signal anxiety*, as Freud called it, spurred the ego to defend against the impulse or situation that threatened to recreate a childhood trauma. Different neuroses were now hypothesized to reflect different psychosexual conflicts and defense mechanisms.

Although psychodynamic theory has not directly produced a general taxonomy analogous to the Kraepelinian system, it has shaped the definitions of disorders in several Kraepelinian taxonomies. Kraepelin (1915) himself discussed psychodynamic variables in hysteria, although he thought they were, at most, secondary to an underlying disease process.

Freud's theory of neurosis had a heavy impact on *DSM*-I and the GAP taxonomy. The *DSM*-I defined psychoneurotic disorders as follows:

> The chief characteristic of these disorders is "anxiety" which may be directly felt and expressed or which may be unconsciously and automatically controlled by the utilization of various psychological defense mechanisms (depression, conversion, displacement, etc.). . . .
>
> "Anxiety" in psychoneurotic disorders is a danger signal felt and perceived by the conscious portion of the personality. It is produced by a threat from within the personality (e.g., by supercharged repressed emotions, including such aggressive impulses as hostility and resentment), with or without stimulation from such external situations as loss of love, loss of prestige, or threat of injury. (APA 1952, pp. 31-32)

Despite the GAP's (1966, p. 209) claim that its approach was "clinical-descriptive" and that it "attempted to set forth operational descriptions," its definition of psychoneurotic disorders relied even more heavily on Freudian inferences:

> This category is reserved for those disorders based on unconscious conflicts over the handling of sexual and aggressive impulses which, though removed from awareness by the mechanism of repression, remain active and unresolved. . . .
>
> The anxiety, acting as a danger signal to the ego, ordinarily sets into operation certain defense mechanisms, in addition to repression, and leads to the formulation of psychological symptoms which symbolically deal with the conflict, thus achieving a partial though unhealthy solution. (GAP, 1966, pp. 229-230)

From the 1930s through the 1960s there was also a widespread psychodynamic presumption against childhood depression, because true depressions were thought to require full internalization of the superego during adolescence (see Kashani et al., 1981).

Current Status of the Psychodynamic Paradigm

After temporarily dictating the definitions of certain disorders in Kraepelinian taxonomies, psychodynamic theory became less evident in *DSM*-II (APA, 1968) and was omitted from *DSM*-III. Even the term "neurosis" was omitted from *DSM*-III until the final draft, when psychodynamically oriented psychiatrists got the term inserted parenthetically beside anxiety disorders: for example, "Anxiety States (or Anxiety Neuroses)."

For childhood disorders, Anna Freud (1965) proposed a Developmental Profile based on the concept of *developmental lines*—the developmental sequences postulated by psychoanalytic theory, such as the oral, anal, and phallic phases of libidinal development (Freud, 1980). Beside libidinal development, she advocated judging children's ego and superego development; the stability of borders between id, ego, and superego; progress from primitive, id-dominated (primary process) thinking to rational, ego-dominated (secondary process) thinking; and progress from seeking immediate gratification (the pleasure principle) to delaying gratification in the interests of adaptation (the reality principle).

The Developmental Profile consists of psychodynamic inferences about drive development (libido and aggression); ego and superego development; regressions and fixations; and conflicts. It culminates in diagnostic categorizations such as the following:

(1) In spite of current behavior disturbance, personality growth is within the wide range of "normality."
(2) Symptoms are of a transitory nature and can be classed as by-products of developmental strain.
(3) There is a permanent drive regression to fixation points that leads to neurotic conflicts.
(4) There is drive regression plus ego and superego regressions that lead to infantilisms, borderline psychotic, delinquent, or psychotic disturbances.
(5) There are primary organic deficiencies or early deprivations that distort development and produce retarded, defective, and nontypical personalities.
(6) There are destructive processes at work of organic, toxic, or psychic origin that have caused or are about to cause a disruption of mental growth. (Adapted from Freud, 1965, p. 147)

This approach differs markedly from the Kraepelinian paradigm, in that it dismisses descriptions in favor of theoretical inferences about psychological functioning and categorizes disorders according to the depth of inferred psychopathology. Despite frequent citations in the child analytic literature, however, there is little evidence for the reliability or validity of the Developmental Profile. Instead, most publications merely illustrate its application to a single child (e.g., Yorke, 1980).

Because the Developmental Profile requires such complex inferences, simpler versions have been proposed. The Metapsychological Assessment Profile, for example, consists of eleven categories rated as good, fair, marginal, or inadequate (Greenspan, Hatleberg, & Cullander, 1980). The categories include ego flexibility, superego functioning, affects, and defenses. Although ratings are more appropriate for reliability analyses than are entries on the Developmental Profile, Greenspan et al. confined their presentation to a single case example, with no reliability or validity data.

Key Questions

Psychoanalytic theory helped to shape the *DSM*-I and GAP taxonomies. The waning of its influence, however, leaves Anna Freud's Developmental Profile as the main legacy of the psychodynamic approach to the taxonomy of child and adolescent disorders. Unlike Kraepelinian taxonomy, the psychodynamic approach subordinates description to a theory of unconscious psychological mechanisms. Psychodynamic taxonomy is based on conclusions that are more akin to idiographic personality formulations than to formal diagnoses. This raises the following questions:

(1) Can the inferences required by psychodynamic theory be made reliably and validly?
(2) How can idiographic formulations of psychodynamics provide a basis for taxonomy?
(3) How can we determine the relevance of psychodynamics to less inferential definitions of disorders?

THE MULTIVARIATE TAXONOMIC PARADIGM

Long before Kraepelinian taxonomies differentiated among disorders of childhood, there were empirical efforts to identify patterns of children's behavior problems. Ackerson (1931), for example, employed

a 125-item list to record the presence versus absence of behavior problems in the case histories of children seen in a guidance clinic. To assess
relations between pairs of items, he later correlated each item with every
other item (Ackerson, 1942). Although the correlation coefficients
showed the quantitative covariation between pairs of items, the 7750
correlations for each sex presented too massive an information-
processing task for the unaided human mind.

To derive syndromes from this mass of data, Jenkins and Glickman
(1946) picked out pairs of highly correlated items and then added items
that correlated highest with each member of the correlated pairs. They
used a combination of statistical criteria and clinical judgment to decide
when to stop adding items to each syndrome. Additional studies by
Jenkins and his colleagues influenced the choice of categories for the
DSM-II behavior disorders of childhood (APA, 1968). Although empirical research thus contributed to the formulation of these categories, the
research data themselves were case history reports, and the analyses did
not provide clinically applicable operational definitions. Furthermore,
rather than being derived directly from the research, the *DSM*-II categories were descriptions of the committee's concepts of the disorders
suggested by the findings.

Multivariate Methods

The Jenkins studies pioneered the use of statistics to aggregate data
on children's behavior problems. However, as electronic computers and
more powerful statistical techniques became available, more formal
multivariate analyses were applied to an increasing range of data on
children's behavior disorders. Most multivariate analyses use correlations to measure the covariation between attributes. Once the correlations among characteristics have been computed, multivariate analyses
use mathematical criteria to detect groups of attributes that covary.
Subjective judgment is involved in selecting the samples and attributes
to be analyzed, the analytic methods, and the mathematical criteria.
Once these choices are made, however, multivariate analyses assess the
covariation among attributes in a perfectly reliable way. Thus, given a
particular set of scores, a particular multivariate analysis should always
produce the same results, no matter who does the analysis. This avoids
the unreliability arising when people mentally aggregate assessment
data into taxonomic judgments.

Multivariate methods have been used mainly to detect covariation
among attributes, although (as discussed later) they can also be used to

construct typologies of individuals. The use of multivariate methods to
detect covariation among attributes is analogous to the efforts of early
nosologists to detect disease entities via clinical descriptions of abnormalities. Multivariate methods, however, can greatly facilitate detection
of patterns among attributes that are variable from one time or situation
to another. Almost any attribute—including observed behavior, test
scores, self-reports, physical parameters, and psychodynamic inferences—
can be subjected to multivariate analysis.

Factor Analysis

Factor analysis is one widely used family of methods for identifying
groups of covarying attributes. It derives dimensions, called *factors,*
from correlations among sets of items that have all been scored for a
group of subjects. Qualitative items can be analyzed by scoring them 0
for absent and 1 for present, but analyses can be made more sensitive by
scoring gradations, even as coarse as 0 for never, 1 for sometimes, and 2
for often. A factor consists of a list of *loadings* for all the items analyzed.
A loading is like a correlation coefficient that can range from –1.00 to
+1.00. An item's loading on a factor shows how highly the item
correlates with the dimension defined by the factor.

Most factor analyses produce several factors, each reflecting covariation among different subsets of items. When used to identify disorders,
items that have high loadings on a particular factor can be viewed as a
syndrome in the literal sense of attributes that tend to occur together.
Items whose loadings on a factor exceed a particular cutoff point, such
as .30, can be employed to define the syndrome.

Cluster Analysis

Cluster analysis is another family of methods for identifying groups
of covarying characteristics. It directly groups items into nondimen-
sional *clusters,* which may intuitively seem more like traditional
syndromes. Yet because each item can belong to only one cluster, cluster
analysis may mask the tendency of some items to covary with two or
more syndromes. Factor analysis, by contrast, reveals such tendencies,
because an item can have a substantial loading on more than one factor.
As a result, some items can be associated with more than one factor-
analytically derived syndrome, just as a symptom such as headache may
be associated with more than one organic disease.

TABLE 4.2
Number of Studies That Have Identified Syndromes
Through Multivariate Analyses

Syndrome	Case Histories	Mental Health Workers	Teachers	Parents	Total
Broad Band					
Overcontrolled	2	1	6	6	15
Undercontrolled	3	3	6	7	19
Pathological Detachment	3	–	1	–	4
Learning Problems	–	–	1	1	2
Narrow Band					
Academic Disability	–	1	–	3	4
Aggressive	3	4	2	8	17
Anxious	1	2	2	2	7
Delinquent	3	1	1	7	12
Depressed	2	1	1	5	9
Hyperactive	3	2	2	7	14
Immature	–	1	1	3	5
Obsessive-Compulsive	1	–	1	2	4
Schizoid	3	4	–	5	12
Sexual Problems	1	2	–	3	6
Sleep Problems	–	–	–	3	3
Social withdrawal	1	1	2	5	9
Somatic Complaints	1	–	–	7	8
Uncommunicative	–	1	–	2	3

SOURCE: From Achenbach and Edelbrock (1978) plus syndromes subsequently identified in factor analyses of the Child Behavior Checklist for boys and girls ages 4-5 and the Teacher's Report Form (Achenbach & Edelbrock, 1983; Edelbrock & Achenbach, 1985).

Syndromes Derived from Multivariate Analyses

Despite differences in rating instruments, subject samples, and analytic methods, multivariate studies have shown considerable convergence on certain syndromes of behavior problems. In a review of 27 studies, Achenbach and Edelbrock (1978) concluded that 18 syndromes had clear counterparts in two or more of the studies. Fourteen syndromes were considered to be "narrow band," analogous to the specific diagnostic categories of Kraepelinian taxonomies, while 4 were "broad band," consisting of items spanning two or more narrow-band syndromes. Table 4.2 shows the number of studies in which versions of each broad- and narrow-band syndrome were found. The names given the syndromes summarize the problems found to occur together. Focusing only on broad-band syndromes, Quay (1979) also concluded that there was considerable convergence between studies. He has since acknowledged that when narrow-band syndromes are viewed as hierarchical subtypes of broad-band syndromes, there is consistency among several narrow-band syndromes as well (Quay, personal communication).

Pointing to differences between the wording of items in different multivariate studies, Lessing, Williams, and Revelle (1981) have questioned whether the findings indeed show much consistency. However, after Achenbach and Edelbrock (1978) had grouped the findings of 27 studies into the categories shown in Table 4.2, other psychologists independently classified 90 percent of the 124 obtained syndromes into the same categories. A study in which parents of disturbed children completed three separate rating instruments also showed significant correlations between nearly all the analogous factor-analytically derived syndromes of the different instruments (Achenbach & Edelbrock, 1983). There is thus substantial consistency between the syndromes obtained with different instruments.

Relations to DSM Syndromes

The narrow-band syndromes derived through multivariate analyses are roughly analogous to the lists of descriptive features specified for *DSM*-III and *DSM*-III-R disorders occurring from the preschool to the adolescent periods. We can therefore compare the descriptive features of the multivariate and *DSM* syndromes, although agreement with formal *DSM* diagnoses may be reduced by the *DSM*'s fixed rules regarding age, duration, number of symptoms, and exclusions. Table 4.3 presents approximate relations between multivariate and *DSM* syndromes. The *DSM* syndromes intended primarily for children and adolescents are listed on the left, with the most closely corresponding multivariate syndromes on the right. The remaining empirically derived syndromes are listed with the most similar *DSM* syndrome in parentheses, even if the *DSM* syndrome was not primarily intended for children or adolescents.

Several *DSM* syndromes have counterparts among the multivariate syndromes, although the following do not: Undersocialized Nonaggressive Conduct Disorder (deleted from *DSM*-III-R); Separation Anxiety Disorders; Avoidant Disorder; Oppositional Disorder; Identity Disorder; and Childhood Onset Pervasive Developmental Disorder. The *DSM*'s Attention Deficit Disorder without Hyperactivity (deleted from *DSM*-III-R) did not have clear counterparts in the studies reviewed by

TABLE 4.3

Approximate Relations between *DSM* and Empirically Derived Syndromes of Childhood Behavior Disorders

DSM	*Empirically Derived Narrow-Band Syndromes*
Attention deficit disorders	
314.01 With hyperactivity	Hyperactive
314.00 Without hyperactivity*	Inattentive (teacher ratings only)
314.80 Residual type	–
Conduct disorders**	
312.00 Undersocialized, aggressive	Aggressive
312.10 Undersocialized, nonaggressive	–
312.23 Socialized, aggressive	Delinquent (boys)
312.21 Socialized, nonaggressive	Delinquent (girls)
312.90 Atypical	–
Anxiety disorders of childhood or adolescence	
309.21 Separation anxiety disorder	–
313.21 Avoidant disorder	–
313.00 Overanxious disorder	Anxious
Other disorders of childhood or adolescence	
313.22 Schizoid disorder	Social withdrawal (?)
313.23 Elective mutism	Uncommunicative
313.81 Oppositional disorder	–
318.82 Identity disorder	–
Pervasive developmental disorders	
299.8 Childhood onset pervasive developmental	–
299.9 Atypical	–
302.60 Gender identity disorder of childhood	Sex problems (boys 4-5)
V62.30 Academic problem	Academic disability
Disorders not specific to childhood or adolescence	
300.30 Obsessive-compulsive disorder	Obsessive-compulsive
300.81 Somatization disorder	Somatic complaints
296.2 Major depressive episode,	Depressed
300.4 Dysthymic disorder,	
309.0 Adjustment disorder	
with depressed mood	
301.22 Schizotypal personality disorder (?)	Schizoid
–	Immature
–	Sexual problems
–	Sleep problems
–	Cruel (girls)

*Deleted from *DSM*-III-R draft.

**DSM*-III-R draft combines all conduct disorders in one category.

Achenbach and Edelbrock (1978) and Quay (1979). However, a syndrome that Quay called "Immaturity" included inattentiveness and was said to be especially evident in special education classes. Subsequent multivariate analyses of teacher ratings have also identified a syndrome characterized largely by inattention (Edelbrock & Achenbach, 1984). Children receiving diagnoses of Attention Deficit Disorder without Hyperactivity have been found to have high scores on this syndrome (Edelbrock, Costello, & Kessler, 1984). The *DSM*'s Residual Attention Deficit Disorder and Atypical Conduct Disorder specify no descriptive features for comparison with multivariate findings.

Broad-Band Versus Narrow-Band Syndromes

The size and nature of the item pool and the method of analysis can affect the number and breadth of the syndromes obtained through multivariate analyses. Analyses of a few dozen relatively molar items, for example, usually produce two or three broad syndromes, whereas analyses of a hundred or more items usually produce from eight to fifteen narrow-band syndromes. Dreger (1981) has even obtained thirty syndromes from a factor analysis of 274 items scored for a heterogeneous sample and using liberal criteria for the retention of factors.

The relations between broad-band syndromes and narrow-band syndromes have been explicated by "second-order" factor analyses of the narrow-band syndromes (Achenbach, 1966, 1978; Achenbach & Edelbrock, 1979, 1983; Miller, 1967). In a second-order factor analysis, scores are first computed for the syndromes derived from ordinary, "first-order" factors. Correlations between these syndrome scores are then factor analyzed to form second-order factors that show which first-order factors are most closely associated with one another. Second-order analyses have shown that narrow-band syndromes of hyperactivity, aggression, and delinquent behavior covary to form a broad-band grouping designated in Table 4.2 as "undercontrolled." This contrasts with a second broad-band grouping composed of depressive, anxious, and somatic problems, designated in Table 4.2 as "overcontrolled."

Although the two broad-band groupings do not subsume all narrow-band syndromes, the second-order analyses show that findings of broad- and narrow-band syndromes are not necessarily contradictory. Instead, they represent different levels of a hierarchy. In his analysis of 274 items, Dreger (1981) carried hierarchical analyses still farther: His second-order analysis of thirty first-order factors yielded nine second-order factors that are similar in breadth to the narrow-band syndromes found in most studies. His third-order analysis of the nine second-order factors yielded four broad-band syndromes.

The second- and third-order findings emphasize that there is not a single "correct" level or number of syndromes. Instead, the degree of differentiation obtained and the utility of a particular level depend on a variety of methodological and pragmatic factors. Broad-band groupings, for example, suggest underlying commonalities among certain narrow-band syndromes, such as excessive anxiety in the overcontrolled syndromes and insufficient anxiety in the undercontrolled syndromes. Broad-band syndromes may also be useful guides for general clinical management, whereas narrow-band syndromes are more useful for training, etiological research, and the choice of specific interventions.

The distinction between narrow- and broad-band multivariate syndromes resembles distinctions between specific syndromes and general categories in Kraepelinian taxonomies, but there are some important differences. The most basic difference is that the broad-band multivariate groupings are derived mathematically from the narrow-band syndromes. There is thus an explicit mathematical relation between the levels, such that the broad-band groupings are defined by correlations between the narrow-band syndromes. The broad-band groupings of Kraepelinian taxonomies, by contrast, are not based on any explicit relations between narrow-band syndromes. Some of the Kraepelinian reliability studies, for example, grouped diverse disorders into a single category called "Other Disorders of Infancy, Childhood, or Adolescence," and all Axis II disorders into "Developmental Disorders" and "Personality Disorders."

From Syndromes to Typologies

Like the syndromes of Kraepelinian taxonomies, those derived from factor analyses and cluster analyses of items represent subsets of problems, rather than a typology of individuals. If syndromes truly represent separate disorders, some individuals might have more than one syndrome, just as a person can have cancer and measles at the same time. However, it is much harder to delimit the boundaries of behavioral syndromes than physical syndromes. DSM-III imposed boundaries by providing differential diagnostic criteria for some disorders and by excluding certain disorders if they are "due to" others. Yet, as discussed earlier, a great deal of overlap was found between some DSM-III categories, such as the Oppositional and Conduct Disorders, with little basis for excluding certain disorders as "due to" others.

The multivariate approach can avoid forced choices between multiple and overlapping categories by scoring the degree to which children manifest the attributes of all relevant syndromes. If each item is scored on a yes/no or multistep scale, a child's scores for all the items of a syndrome can be summed to obtain a total score for that syndrome. Item scores can also be differentially weighted: for example, by multiplying each item's score by its loading on the factor from which a syndrome was derived and then summing these scores to produce a *factor score*. Composite scores of this sort give greatest weight to the items that have the highest factor loadings; that is, the highest correlations with the syndrome defined by the factor.

Whether obtained by a simple sum of item scores or a weighted sum, the scores for each syndrome can be converted to a common metric by transforming them into standard scores, such as Z scores or T scores. When this is done, a particular standard score reflects the same deviation from the mean on each syndrome. By using data from normative samples, standard scores can be constructed to show a child's deviance from the mean for the normative groups. All the syndromes found for children of a particular age and sex can be cast into a profile format. We can then view the child's standing on all syndromes simultaneously and see the areas of greatest and least deviance.

As an example, Figure 4.1 illustrates the Child Behavior Profile, which is designed to score children on syndromes derived from factor analyses of the Child Behavior Checklist. The Checklist has 118 behavior problem items that parents score as 0 for not true of their child; 1 for somewhat or sometimes true; and 2 for very true or often true. To reflect age and sex differences in the prevalence and patterning of behavior problems, separate factor analyses were done for clinically referred children of each sex at ages 4-5, 6-11, and 12-16. The profile in Figure 4.1 is the version for 6-11-year-old boys. To compare a boy with typical boys of the same age, normative samples of 6-11-year-old boys provide the basis for converting raw scores on each scale to the percentiles shown on the left and standard scores (T scores) shown on the right side of the profile. By adding up the scores obtained by a boy on the items of each syndrome and marking the scores in the columns of the graphic display, a profile is formed that compares the boy with a normative sample for each syndrome. The headings "Internalizing" and "Externalizing" at the top of the profile indicate the narrow-band syndromes that are grouped together on second-order factors like those designated as overcontrolled and undercontrolled in Table 4.2.

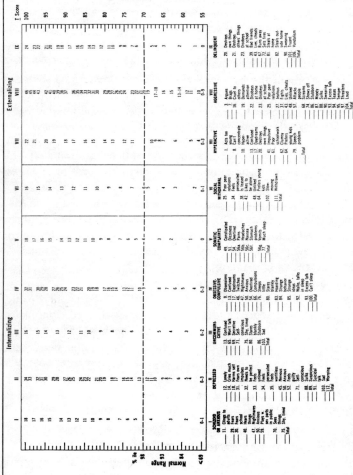

SOURCE: Achenbach and Edelbrock (1983).

Figure 4.1   Example of Profile for Scoring Syndromes Derived Through Multivariate Analyses

Cluster Analysis of Profiles

The scales of the profile shown in Figure 4.1 represent syndromes of cooccurring attributes, many of which have *DSM*-III counterparts. Boys having high scores on the Depressed syndrome of the profile, for example, usually qualify for a *DSM*-III diagnosis of Major Depressive Episode or Dysthymia (Edelbrock, 1984). However, boys who show many depressive features may also be deviant in other areas. The *DSM* can take account of the other areas of deviance only by adding all other diagnoses for which the boy qualifies, as if each one represented a separate disorder. A profile, by contrast, simultaneously displays a child's standing on many syndromes. Groups of children who have similar patterns can be formed by cluster analyzing their profiles.

In this application of cluster analysis, correlations (or other measures of similarity) are computed between each pair of profiles in a sample. The correlation indicates the degree of similarity between one child's profile and another child's profile. Most clustering algorithms start with pairs of individuals having very similar profiles. Larger groupings (clusters) are formed by adding progressively less similar individuals to each pair. In *centroid* cluster analysis, the operational definition of each cluster is the profile formed by averaging all the member profiles of the cluster. This average profile is called the *centroid* of the cluster. The reliability of profile types can be tested by replicating the cluster analysis in a new sample and computing correlations between the centroids obtained in the two samples. The profile types that are significantly correlated in the two samples are deemed to be reliable. Figure 4.2 illustrates the centroids of six profile types found to be reliable in cluster analyses of Child Behavior Profiles for 6-11-year-old boys (for further details, see Achenbach & Edelbrock, 1983; Edelbrock & Achenbach, 1980).

Note that profile Type B has peaks on the Depressed, Social Withdrawal, and Aggressive syndromes. Rather than viewing these three very different syndromes as completely separate disorders, we can thus see that there is a group of boys who share an overall behavior pattern characterized by considerable deviance in all three areas. This does not necessarily mean that all boys who are deviant in one of the areas are also deviant in the other two. Profile Type A in Figure 4.2 shows about the same degree of deviance as Type B on the Social Withdrawal syndrome, for example, but more deviance on the Schizoid syndrome and less on the Depressed and Aggressive syndromes. If we were to classify boys only in terms of the Social Withdrawal syndrome, we would inadevertently include at least two very different groups—those

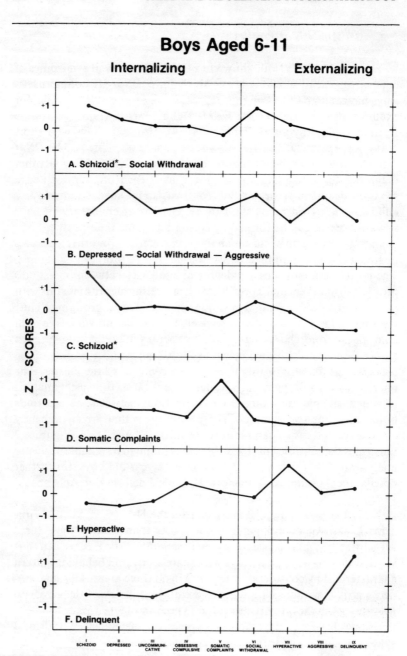

SOURCE: Achenbach and Edelbrock (1983).
*Schizoid or Anxious.

Figure 4.2 Profile Types Found Through Cluster Analysis of the Child
            Behavior Profile

with profile Type A and those with Type B. Failure to consider overall patterns of problems undermines efforts to study children categorized on the basis of a single diagnostic category or unidimensional rating scale, such as those designed to assess hyperactivity or depression. Many of the children who meet the criterion for a particular categorical disorder may be deviant in other areas as well.

Hierarchical Aspects of Typology

When cluster analyses proceed hierarchically from pairs of very similar individuals to progressively larger and less homogeneous clusters, we can compare the clusters emerging at various levels in the hierarchy. This is analogous to comparing narrow- and broad-band syndromes of items obtained in first- and second-order factor analyses. It differs from the hierarchical analysis of syndromes, however, in that the clusters at the lowest levels in the hierarchy consist of relatively small groups of individuals who have very similar profile patterns. The higher-level clusters consist of larger, more heterogeneous groups composed of the most similar of the smaller groups.

When centroid cluster analysis is used, correlations can be computed between an individual's profile and the centroids of profile types at all levels of a hierarchy. Individuals can then be grouped according to the profile types that they most closely resemble. Figure 4.3 illustrates relations between groups of 6-11-year-old boys having the profile patterns shown in Figure 4.2 and the broader grouping formed as the cluster analysis proceeded hierarchically. Like the hierarchy of syndromes, the hierarchy of profile patterns culminates in broad groupings distinguished mainly by a preponderance of "internalizing" versus "externalizing" behaviors. Each box in Figure 4.3 indicates the percentage of clinically referred boys in a sample of 1050 whose profiles most closely resembled each type in the hierarchy.

Although other measures of profile similarity can be used, the *intraclass correlation* was chosen for the analyses shown in Figure 4.3, because it reflects similarity between the individual's profile and the centroid of a profile type in terms of both the patterns of scores and their magnitude. The intraclass correlation can range from -1.00 (perfect negative correlation) to $+1.00$ (perfect similarity in both pattern and magnitude). It has been found to be an especially good measure of similarity between profiles (Edelbrock & McLaughlin, 1980).

Because the intraclass correlation provides an objective, quantitative index of resemblance between a child's profile and each profile type,

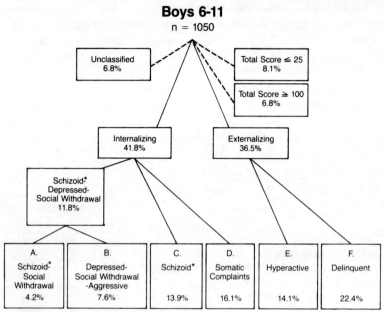

SOURCE: Achenbach and Edelbrock (1983).
NOTE: Percentages indicate percentage of boys classified by each type.
*Schizoid or Anxious.

Figure 4.3 Hierarchical Relations Between Profile Types Found for 6-11-Year-Old Boys

classification can be based on the user's decision about the degree of resemblance to require for membership in a class. If the user seeks very homogeneous groups, a high intraclass correlation can be required for classification into each group. A side effect of a stringent classification criterion, however, is that a large proportion of cases may be left unclassified. If the user prefers more complete coverage of cases at the expense of having less homogeneous groups, a lower intraclass correlation can be chosen for assignment of individuals to the classes of the typology.

The desired degree of resemblance to profile types can be operationalized through the choice of cutoff points for intraclass correlations, and the user can test the effects of various cutoffs on the homogeneity, coverage, and correlates of the classes (for detailed illustrations, see Achenbach & Edelbrock, 1983; Edelbrock, 1979; Edelbrock & Achenbach, 1980). Because global clusters, such as the internalizing and externalizing clusters, are quantitatively derived composites of the more homogeneous clusters, rigorous comparisons can also be made of the utility of each level of classification for specific purposes.

Reliability

In considering the reliability of Kraepelinian taxonomies, we saw that most studies focused on agreement between judges in categorizing cases in which the judges were each exposed to identical assessment data. When categorization depends on the clinician's mental integration of assessment data and subjective judgment of whether a case meets verbally prescribed criteria, this is indeed an appropriate way to test the reliability of the categorization process itself. However, it fails to reflect the potential unreliability of the assessment data on which the judgments are based. Furthermore, because the Kraepelinian taxonomies fail to define their categories in terms of specific assessment operations, no single type of assessment data provides the necessary and sufficient conditions for taxonomic decisions. Of the several types of data relevant to the diagnosis of children's disorders, most involve reports of behavior that does not occur in the clinician's presence, but in the home, school, or neighborhood. Both the reliability and completeness of such data are crucial, though largely neglected, determinants of Kraepelinian diagnostic decisions as they are actually made under clinical conditions.

Unlike the Kraepelinian paradigm, the multivariate paradigm does not require the clinician to mentally integrate diverse data and then make a subjective decision as to whether the child meets verbally prescribed criteria for a taxonomic category. Instead, the multivariate taxonomic process employs standardized procedures to obtain assessment data that are then integrated mathematically. Subjective decisions are involved in the development of assessment and taxonomic procedures and the selection of certain parameters, such as cutoff points. Once the procedures are established, however, a particular set of assessment data should always produce exactly the same taxonomic results. The main reliability questions, therefore, concern the assessment data that serve as input.

Reliability of Syndrome Scores

Numerous studies have reported the reliability and stability of scores for multivariate syndromes. Table 4.4 presents a summary of these

TABLE 4.4
Reliability and Stability of Ratings in Multivariate Studies

Type of Measure	Type of Rater	Type of Syndrome	
		Narrow-Band	Broad-Band
Test-Retest reliability (1 week to 1 month)	Parents	.88	.90
	Teachers	.85	.88
Short-term stability (1½ to 6 months)	Parents	.77	.83
	Teachers	.71	.77
	Mental Health Workers	.65	.69
Long-term stability (15 months to 5 years)	Parents	.52	.60
Interrater reliability	Parents	.69	.69
	Teachers		.79
	Mental Health Workers	.72	
Different raters seeing children in different contexts		.19	.37

SOURCES: Averages computed for z-transformed Pearson correlations in studies reported by Achenbach and Edelbrock (1978, 1981, 1983); Edelbrock and Achenbach (1985); Edelbrock, Greenbaum, & Conover, (1985).

findings for data from parents, teachers, and mental health workers for broad-band and narrow-band syndromes. The findings are summarized in terms of the averages of correlations between the scores obtained from pairs of raters or the same raters on two occasions.

Because all the correlations are based on the Pearson r, they reflect primarily the similarities in the *rank ordering* of scores. This means that two sets of scores could correlate highly but differ in magnitude if one rater always used lower scores than the other. In those studies that provided sufficient data for comparison of the magnitude of scores, there were no consistent differences in mean scores between two types of informants (e.g., mothers versus fathers) who rated children at the same time. In test-retest ratings by the same informant on two occasions, however, behavior problem scores usually declined from the first to the second occasion. Where the ratings were repeated over a relatively brief interval (one week to one month), the decline in scores generally was too small to affect the taxonomic results. They were consistent enough even in normal samples, however, to suggest a general tendency for raters to report less problem behavior on repeated ratings over periods too brief for actual behavioral changes to occur (Achenbach & Edelbrock, 1983; Evans, 1975; Milich, Roberts, Loney, & Caputo, 1980). Over longer periods (six weeks to five years), larger decreases in behavior problem scores were found in most samples. These decreases are more likely to reflect true declines in perceived problem behavior, as a function of treatment, regression effects, and/or development.

Unlike the reliability studies of Kraepelinian taxonomies discussed earlier, most of the paired raters were not exposed to identical data about each child. Instead, the pairs of teachers typically saw the children in different classes in which environmental conditions and the teachers themselves might evoke different behaviors. Although there may have been more overlap between the environments in which pairs of parents and pairs of mental health workers saw the children, there could have been real differences in the children's reactions to each rater when the other rater was not present. Where there were major differences between both the type of rater (e.g., parent versus teacher versus clinician) and type of environment (e.g., home versus school versus clinic), the correlations were lower than for any other combination in Table 4.4. This no doubt reflects differences in the judgmental standards of different types of informants, as well as differences in the child's behavior occurring in their presence. Integration of differing and conflicting assessment data is a key problem for all approaches to taxonomy that Chapter 6 will address.

Reliability of Profile Types

There has been much less research on the reliability of assignment of individuals to profile types. However, a comparison has been made of profile types scored from Child Behavior Checklists completed by mothers of clinically referred children and by a psychologist who interviewed the children and families and examined Checklist ratings by the parents, teachers, and children themselves (Edelbrock & Achenbach, 1980). Because she had access to the mothers' ratings, the psychologist's judgments were not independent of the mothers'. The data considered by the psychologist and mothers, however, differed more than those considered by pairs of diagnosticians in the reliability studies of Kraepelinian taxonomies, as the psychologist's ratings were based on data from several additional sources, as well as her judgment of the mothers' accuracy. When profiles were categorized according to the cluster-analytic typology, categorizations derived from the psychologist's and mothers' ratings averaged 74 percent agreement for the differentiated profile types and 83 percent for more global types (internalizing, externalizing, and, for some groups, a mixed type). The kappas were .64 for the differentiated profile types and .62 for the global types.

Validity

According to the passage quoted earlier from Spitzer and Cantwell (1980), face validity was an important consideration in the definition of *DSM*-III's child and adolescent categories. For variables that are completely self-evident, face valid assessment may be easy and sufficient. For example, if we want to know whether children can name the days of the week, asking them to name the days of the week would be a face valid assessment procedure. However, child and adolescent behavior disorders are not so susceptible to self-evident definition and face valid assessment. Although direct observations of certain specific problem behaviors may seem face valid, it is harder to delimit boundaries between the normal and the pathological or between different types of disorders. The lack of either self-evident or well-validated operational definitions for childhood disorders rules out face validity or correlation with a single definitive criterion as a basis for validating multivariate syndromes. Instead, validation of empirically derived syndromes requires psychometric "bootstrapping"—that is, finding relations between multivariate syndromes derived in different ways and also between multivariate syndromes and other important variables.

Several studies have shown significant correlations between syndromes scored from different instruments (see Achenbach & Edelbrock, 1978, 1983). Where a single instrument was factor analyzed for several different populations, similar factors have been found (see Achenbach & Edelbrock, 1978; Quay, 1979). Furthermore, when a rating instrument was designed to test previously obtained syndromes via confirma-

TABLE 4.5
Syndromes Verified Through Confirmatory Multivariate Analyses

Aggressive
Attentional Problems with Hyperactivity
Anxious-Depressed
Cruel (girls only)
Delinquent
Obsessive-Compulsive
Schizoid-Thought Disorder
Sex Problems
Socially Inept
Somatic Complaints
Uncommunicative-Withdrawn

SOURCE: From Achenbach, Conners, and Quay (1985).

tory factor analyses of new samples, the syndromes listed in Table 4.5 were solidly confirmed (Achenbach, Conners, & Quay, 1985).

The multivariate syndromes have also shown discriminative validity in terms of their differential correlates. Children manifesting broad-band undercontrolled syndromes, for example, have less adequate families, are less socially competent, have worse prognoses, and are less appropriate candidates for psychotherapy than children manifesting overcontrolled syndromes (Achenbach & Edelbrock, 1978). Other studies have reported correlations between both narrow- and broad-band syndromes and numerous other variables, such as independently assessed attention deficits with and without hyperactivity, impulsivity, gender disturbance, depression, firesetting, epilepsy, conduct problems, parental characteristics, child abuse, and ego functioning (see Achenbach & Edelbrock, 1983; Quay, 1979). Classification of children according to profile types has also shown significant discrimination with respect to other variables, such as social competencies and demographic characteristics (Achenbach & Edelbrock, 1983; Langner, Gersten, & Eisenberg, 1974).

A further form of validation has been the demonstration that children whose behavior was independently judged to be deviant had significantly higher syndrome scores than children considered to be normal. When children referred for mental health services were compared to demographically matched nonreferred children, for example, the referred children have shown significantly higher scores on both broad- and narrow-band syndromes in American, Chilean, and Dutch studies (Achenbach & Edelbrock, 1983; Montenegro, 1983; Verhulst, 1985).

Key Questions

The multivariate paradigm employs statistical procedures to identify groups of attributes that tend to cooccur. Like Kraepelin, it aims to differentiate between disorders on the basis of descriptive characteristics. Multivariate methods can objectively integrate a far greater volume of highly variable data than the unaided human mind. They can therefore aid in deriving taxonomies of disorders that lack salient physical features and dramatically abnormal behavior. Although multivariate methods are quantitative, they are not restricted to "dimensional" representations of disorders. Instead, highly correlated items can be treated as syndromal categories, cutoff points can be used to impose categories on continuous distributions of scores, and cluster analyses can form groups of similar individuals. Like all methods, however, multivariate methods are constrained by the type of data analyzed. They have usually been applied to a single class of data, such as ratings by parents, teachers, or mental health workers. Because the taxonomic results are mathematically derived from the data, assessment is rigorously linked to taxonomy. Nevertheless, the dependence of multivariate taxonomy on a particular assessment method raises the following questions:

(1) How can multivariate descriptions be linked to other relevant criteria, such as the age of the child and duration of the problems?
(2) How can multivariate taxonomy integrate data from different sources, such as ratings by different informants, direct observations, clinical interviews, and medical and psychological tests?
(3) How can the quantitative relations captured by multivariate methods be used to improve upon traditional concepts of disorders?

LACK OF A BEHAVIORAL TAXONOMIC PARADIGM

The taxonomic paradigms discussed so far have direct counterparts in three of the four major assessment paradigms discussed in Chapter 2: Kraepelinian taxonomy is derived from the medical assessment paradigm; psychodynamic assessment and taxonomy are both derived from psychoanalytic theory; psychometric assessment and multivariate taxonomy are both based on statistical methodology.

Behavioral assessment, however, lacks a clear taxonomic counter-part. Why? As we saw in Chapter 2, the principles of behavioral assessment are stated largely as contrasts with "traditional" medical, psycho-dynamic, and psychometric assessment. A primary basis for the contrasts is that traditional assessment is said to focus on inferred constructs, whereas behavioral assessment focuses on observable behaviors.

Although it is true that psychodynamic assessment focuses almost exclusively on inferred constructs, both medical and psychometric assessment seek accurate descriptions of observable behavior. The ultimate goal of medical assessment is to identify organic abnormalities, but psychometric assessment involves a general methodology that is not necessarily limited to inferred entities. Psychometric methodology can be applied to behavioral observations, and some behavioral assessors have stressed the need for doing so (e.g., Hartmann, 1983; Patterson, 1981). Others have been concerned with aggregating molecular behaviors into higher-order units. Robert Wahler, for example, has identified clusters of behaviors that covary over time in individual children, such as a child whose work on school assignments correlated positively with self-stimulatory behaviors and social interactions (Wahler, Berland, & Coe, 1979; Wahler & Fox, 1980). In discussing behavioral assessment of social skills, McFall (1982, p. 11) maintains that

> the molecular model fails as a guide because it makes an explicit attempt to avoid the use of theoretical constructs by reducing behavior to its most elementary units. Of course, there can be no escape, since even the most molecular behavioral unit is a construction of the scientist who uses it.
>
> The molecular model, with its emphasis on specificity and its distrust of general classifications, has tended to back itself into an extreme and indefensible position. Specificity can be carried only so far and classification cannot be avoided. Each event cannot be treated as unique. The real issue is not whether classification is good, but what units of classification are most useful for assessment and prediction. The issue is to be resolved empirically.

Not all behavioral assessors agree, however. Nelson (1983, p. 195), for example, argues that because "psychometric criteria are largely incompatible with behavioral assumptions," standardized psychometrically sound behavioral assessment is "unattainable and undesirable." In proclaiming the independence of behavioral assessment from psychometric concerns, she simultaneously seems to reject taxonomic concerns, as she refers to the *DSM* taxonomies as "traditional *assessment* techniques" (p. 196, italics added). Eschewal of the distinction between assessment and taxonomy may be due to a lack of behavioral concepts for aggregates of cooccurring behaviors:

> Behavior therapy has no concept clearly analogous to that of a syndrome. Behavioral treatments are likely to focus on symptoms (target behaviors). ... There is a lack of attention to the possibility that larger constellations of behavior may need to be assessed and treated.
>
> Within behavior therapy, there is little appreciation for the fact that behaviors often come in packages or that constellations have been demonstrated empirically in many multivariate analyses. Behavioral assessment infrequently attempts to determine whether the target behavior for a given client is part of a larger scheme of behaviors, cognitions, and affect. (Kazdin, 1983, pp. 84-85)

Because psychometric methodology is not restricted to particular theories or definitions of the target variables, it can be applied to behavioral assessment. Decisions are required, however, as to what aspects of behavior are appropriate for standardized assessment and what aspects are too idiosyncratic to warrant standardization. Such choices are required for the aggregation of any characteristics across individuals. To accumulate and communicate knowledge about the most effective interventions for particular problems, behavioral assessment needs to be linked to reliable and valid taxonomic distinctions (Mash, 1985). The distinctions need not be those of existing Kraepelinian, psychodynamic, or multivariate taxonomies, but some type of taxonomic scheme is needed for communication, research, training, and the accumulation of knowledge. As demonstrated by the multivariate syndromes, psychometric methodology is general and open-ended enough for application to behavioral data without necessarily sacrificing the strengths of behavioral approaches to unvalidated aspects of "traditional" approaches.

OTHER APPROACHES TO TAXONOMY

Service-Based Taxonomies

Numerous taxonomies are used to guide services in institutional and bureaucratic contexts. Some of these are purely practical guides to management that coexist with other taxonomies. A residential treatment center, for example, may classify children according to their self-help skills and suicide risk, independently of their diagnostic categorization.

Psychoeducational taxonomies originated with efforts to identify mentally retarded children for special classes around the turn of the century. With the advent of IQ tests, the IQ became a criterion for assignment to programs ranging from those for trainable and educable retarded children to those for gifted children. By the 1960s, psychoeducational distinctions were used to assign increasingly differentiated services for perceptual-motor handicaps, learning disabilities, economic and linguistic disadvantages, and social-emotional disturbance. A reaction against all forms of special education and "labeling" in the 1970s spawned the ideal of mainstreaming and legal mandates for least restrictive environments. Taxonomic efforts were thus rejected at the same time as an increasing variety of special help was demanded. The resulting dilemmas were studied by a panel of experts in the Project on the Classification of Exceptional Children, sponsored by ten federal agencies (Hobbs, 1975). Many of the contributors opposed labeling children, but they acknowledged the need for classification in the assignment of services.

Beside the risk of stigmatizing children, service-based taxonomies sometimes obstruct services for children who do not conform neatly to their categories (Nagi, 1980). A child who meets criteria for emotional disturbance, for example, may thereby become ineligible for services to the learning disabled and vice versa, even though the same child may have both problems. Such categories may be based more on political or bureaucratic considerations than on children's actual needs. Inadequate resources may also prompt unduly narrow interpretations of criteria for costly services.

The Ecological Approach

One approach to service-based classification is ecological assessment of the interactions between children and their environments (Salzinger, Antrobus, & Glick, 1980). Ecological assessment aims to identify functional relations between specific environments and behaviors considered problematic in those environments, rather than viewing problems as intrinsic to the child. Labeling a child as "inattentive" in school, for example, may reflect a clash between the child's and the school's agendas, rather than an attention deficit intrinsic to the child.

Like behavioral approaches, the ecological approach emphasizes the situational specificity of behavior. As an illustration, Hobbs (1980) proposed an "ecologically oriented, service-based classification system" for handicapped children. This entails an "audit of assets and deficits in the child's ecosystem with respect to requirements for service." A plan is then devised for obtaining services required for the child to progress toward developmental goals. The basic procedure for assessing the child's service requirements is a conference attended by relevant professionals, significant others, and the child (if old enough). The conference is to agree on the child's needs and on a person to ensure that each one is met.

The procedure proposed by Hobbs resembles the interdisciplinary formulation of individual education plans (IEPs) required by Public Law 94-142, Education for All Handicapped Children. Hobbs acknowledged, however, that it is "altogether inadequate for research and for epidemiological and demographic studies" (1980, p. 285). It is also doubtful that such a procedure fulfills any taxonomic functions. Getting all the involved parties together is a worthy goal to counteract bureaucratic obstacles, but what is done often reflects the differing agendas of the participants, more than a data-based selection of the best means for helping children (Sarason & Klaber, 1985).

COGNITIVE ECONOMICS OF TAXONOMIC PARADIGMS

People devise taxonomies to help them simplify large quantities of information. All approaches to taxonomy selectively abstract a few of the many attributes that characterize individuals or disorders. Where etiologies are unknown, taxonomies constitute hypotheses about how best to conceptualize problem behavior. Such taxonomies are always provisional, subject to change as warranted by new needs, ideas, and data. Taxonomies are neither right nor wrong, but should be judged according to how effectively they organize information, promote communication, guide the search for knowledge, and facilitate decisions about individuals. Like assessment paradigms, the major taxonomic paradigms differ with respect to their main strengths and vulnerabilities. Here we will compare and contrast their vulnerabilities to information-processing biases, as summarized in Table 4.6.

TABLE 4.6
Sources of Information-Processing Biases
in Major Taxonomic Paradigms

	Paradigms		
Sources of Bias	*Kraepelinian*	*Psychodynamic*	*Multivariate*
Illusory correlation	categorical concepts imply correlations that may be illusory	theory implies correlations that may be illusory	–
Inability to assess covariation	relies on clinical concepts of disorders rather than assess-ment of covariation	relies on theory of personality rather than assessment of covariation	–
Representativeness heuristic	disease concept	idiographic fallacy	nomothetic fallacy
Availability heuristic	a priori categories	–	–
Confirmatory bias	assumption of specific entity to be found	subordinates descrip-tion to theoretical assumptions	–
Other limitations	lack of operational basis for obtaining and integrating assessment data	lack of explicit criteria for discriminating between taxa	reliance on one type of assessment data

Illusory Correlation

The unstructured descriptions of disorders in pre-*DSM*-III Kraepe-linian taxonomies and *DSM*-III's lists of descriptive criteria imply that the descriptive features tend to occur together. For some disorders, *DSM*-III provided two or more lists of descriptive features that jointly defined the disorder. For Attention Deficit Disorders, for example, five items were listed under each of the headings of "Inattention" and "Hyperactivity," and six under the heading of "Impulsivity." This implied covariation among the members of each list defining a compo-nent of a larger syndrome. The larger syndrome, in turn, was defined by the cooccurrence of members of two of the lists for Attention Deficit without Hyperactivity and all three lists for Attention Deficit with Hyperactivity.

The *DSM*-III criteria for childhood disorders were not derived from correlations between either the specific items or the components defined by the separate lists. Furthermore, some items bore little relation to other items listed under a particular heading. "Has difficulty organizing work" and "needs a lot of supervision," for example, were both listed under Impulsivity, but could refer to behaviors that have little in common with the concept of impulsivity or other members of the list. Problems also arise from having multiple items refer to the same behavior. "Has difficulty sticking to a play activity" and "shifts excessively from one activity to another," for example, could refer to exactly the same behavior, even though the first was listed under Inattention, whereas the second was listed under Impulsivity. Indeed, a factor analysis of mothers' and teachers' ratings of the ADD items showed that the four items just quoted all loaded on an Inattention factor, rather than the separate factors implied by *DSM*-III (Pelham, Atkins, Murphy, & White, 1981). The draft of *DSM*-III-R replaces the three lists of items with a single list, but the list was not derived from direct empirical assessment of covariation among the items.

The psychodynamic definitions in the GAP taxonomy and Anna Freud's Developmental Profile imply correlations that have not been empirically verified. The Developmental Profile, for example, states that cleanliness, orderliness, punctuality, hoarding, and doubt betray difficulty with impulses of the anal-sadistic phase (Freud, 1965, pp. 144-145).

The multivariate paradigm is not vulnerable to illusory correlation, because its syndromes are based on empirically measured correlations, although there is a risk that different methods of data collection and analysis can yield different correlations and syndromes.

Inability to Assess Covariation

When taxa are constructed by asking clinicians to describe their concepts of disorders (e.g., Spitzer & Cantwell, 1980), there is no provision for assessing the actual covariation among the defining criteria. The lack of operational definitions for the descriptive criteria also precludes objective assessment of covariation, although many of the descriptive criteria could be defined operationally via assessment procedures such as rating forms, interviews, or direct observations. When such procedures have been used to make *DSM* diagnoses, however, they usually have categorized children according to the existing *DSM* criteria without assessing actual covariation among the criteria (e.g., Costello et al., 1984).

The psychodynamic paradigm makes no provision for assessing covariation in either the initial definition of disorders or the subsequent diagnosis of individuals. The multivariate paradigm, on the other hand, derives its syndromes and types directly from empirically assessed covariation. Furthermore, objective quantitative procedures can be used to determine the resemblance of individual cases to multivariate syndromes and profile types.

The Representativeness Heuristic

The representativeness heuristic affects the three taxonomic paradigms in ways that parallel its effects on the three corresponding assessment paradigms, as discussed in Chapter 2. According to the original Kraepelinian paradigm, each syndrome of signs and symptoms represents a disease. Although even Kraepelin eventually gave up the assumption that each entity must reflect organic abnormalities, his paradigm continues to imply that deviant behaviors are to be understood as representative of specific categorical disorders. If the goal of the taxonomic process is to match a child's presenting picture to a particular category, assessment is apt to concentrate on attributes that define and differentiate between preexisting categories. Once a category is selected, the child's problems may be viewed as representative of or "explained by" that category. Children who meet the criteria for a particular category may also be viewed as a homogeneous group, even though the lack of operational definitions for current Kraepelinian taxonomies and the variety of ways to meet the criteria permit considerable variation between such children.

Psychodynamic taxonomy is based on a theory of personality. The psychodynamic definitions of neurosis in the GAP taxonomy and Anna Freud's (1965) diagnostic categories imply that there are classes of children who share complex underlying psychodynamics despite differences in their symptoms. Insofar as taxonomic criteria are stated at all, they concern instinctual drives and personality structures inferred from idiographic assessment. The absence of taxonomic criteria that can be uniformly applied across cases leaves the idiographic portrayal of personality as the main basis for taxonomic decisions. This presents a difficult task for taxa such as Anna Freud's diagnostic category D, which is defined as follows: "There is drive regression plus . . . simultaneous ego and superego regressions which lead to infantilisms, borderline, delinquent, or psychotic disturbances" (Freud, 1965, p. 147). Such categories require a chain of subjective inferences not only about the child's personality but also about the multiple possibilities included in each taxon.

In Chapter 2 we used the term "idiographic fallacy" for personality interpretations viewed as representative of an individual's functioning across time and situations or as representative of a class of similar people. The term idiographic fallacy also applies to the specification of taxonomic categories in terms of idiographic personality portraits without explicit criteria for class membership. The complex, inferential nature of such categories makes them vulnerable to information-processing biases arising from the representativeness heurisic, as discussed in Chapter 1.

Just as the idiographic fallacy threatens psychodynamic assessment and taxonomy, the opposite tendency, termed the "nomothetic fallacy," may threaten multivariate taxonomy as well as psychometric assessment. ("Nomothetic" refers to general laws, in contrast to individual patterns.) Whereas psychodynamic assessment and taxonomy focus on the inferred particulars of personality, multivariate taxonomy and psychometric assessment focus on attributes measured uniformly across individuals.

Once a multivariate taxonomy has been constructed, its criteria depend on a specific set of assessment procedures, scoring rules, and normative data. This makes it hard to add new attributes or syndromes that were not included in the original standardization. Furthermore, the statistical basis for multivariate taxonomy may make it hard to detect rare syndromes in the initial construction process. Infantile autism, for example, would not have been detected through multivariate analyses of heterogeneous clinical samples, unless they contained enough autistic children and were scored for hallmarks of autism that probably would not have been included in standardized assessment before the clinical concept of autism was introduced.

The problem of unfamiliar phenomena also affects nonstatistical approaches, as indicated by the 37 years elapsing between Leo Kanner's (1943) classic description of infantile autism and its addition to the *DSM* (APA, 1980), five years after multivariate methods had been used to discriminate autism from other severe developmental deviations (Prior, Perry, & Gajzago, 1975).

The representativeness heuristic can bias judgments based on multivariate taxonomy if all the attributes embodied in the taxa are viewed as literally representative of individual children. Because each taxon is derived from statistical associations among features assessed across many children, few or no children may actually possess every feature of a taxon. This is especially true for the syndromes of items derived through factor analysis. Such syndromes reflect the covariation of items across children, but not necessarily "types" of children. Consequently, there may be no children who manifest all the attributes having high loadings on a factor. Furthermore, even if most of the high loading attributes of a syndrome are reported for a child, we cannot necessarily assume that the other attributes are really present, though unreported, or that they will emerge. Either of these possibilities may, in fact, be true, but the quantitative nature of multivariate syndromes implies that they exist in degrees rather than being defined as totally present if certain criteria are met, but totally absent if the criteria are not met.

Similarly, a profile type derived through cluster analysis represents an average of a group of statistically similar profiles. There may thus be no child who has a profile identical to the average profile that operationally defines the type. Instead, resemblance to a type is a matter of degree, and a child may resemble more than one type to some degree. The representativeness heuristic can be a source of bias when people unduly impose categorical concepts on quantitatively assessed phenomena, either in their conceptualization of "types" of disorders or in their view of an individual child's problems.

The Availability Heuristic

Kraepelinian taxonomies are probably the most vulnerable to the availability heuristic, because they depend so heavily on mental matching of individual cases to a priori categories. By providing so few categories for childhood disorders, pre-1960s Kraepelinian taxonomies intrinsically imposed a harsh availability bias. However, in more differentiated taxonomies, such as the GAP and *DSM*-III, availability biases stem from the difficulty of giving equal weight to all criteria and all categories of disorders when judging individual cases. If we are especially attuned to conduct disorders, for example, or if initial information about a child suggests a conduct disorder, it may be hard to give equal weight to criteria for oppositional and attention deficit disorders, especially when there is so much overlap among children meeting the criteria for these three classes of disorders (Costello et al., 1984).

For different reasons, psychodynamic and multivariate taxonomies may be less vulnerable to the availability heuristic. Although the psychodynamic paradigm provides only a limited range of taxonomic alternatives, its idiographic orientation downplays taxonomy so much that its a priori taxa are not very salient. The multivariate paradigm avoids the availability heuristic by simultaneously scoring standardized assessment data in a uniform fashion for all taxa. There is thus no mental weighting of assessment data or mental matching of cases to categories.

The Confirmatory Bias

In Kraepelinian taxonomies, confirmatory biases are apt to arise from the assumption that each child's deviance can be explained in terms of one or more categorical disorders. This assumption about the nature of deviance may promote overweighting of data that appear to confirm such disorders, to the neglect of conflicting data. It may thus be hard to entertain alternative conceptions of deviance, such as multidimensional patterns that do not conform to the Kraepelinian model.

The vulnerability of the psychodynamic paradigm stems from the precedence it gives to theoretical assumptions and symbolic interpretations over explicit descriptive data. Because psychoanalysts such as Anna Freud (1965) have maintained that observable behavioral problems are less important than inferred dynamics, the psychodynamic paradigm does not offer a basis for making taxonomic distinctions independent of theoretical interpretations. The data sought and the interpretations made are therefore especially susceptible to confirmatory biases.

Because the multivariate paradigm derives taxonomic distinctions directly from standardized assessment data, it should not be vulnerable to confirmatory biases in the data obtained or in the weighting of data.

Other Limitations

Beside information-processing biases, certain other limitations affect the taxonomic paradigms. Kraepelinian taxonomies of childhood disorders, for example, are limited by their lack of operational procedures for obtaining and integrating assessment data. Because neither the categories nor the specific criteria for each category were derived from empirical research, it is not clear how well the actual characteristics of child and adolescent disorders are captured. Furthermore, the lack of operational criteria makes the choice and evaluation of assessment data largely arbitrary. Although the *DSM* now provides more explicit criteria than earlier Kraepelinian taxonomies, its failure to specify procedures for integrating diverse data is a continuing source of vulnerability to bias.

The psychodynamic paradigm suffers from a similar lack of empirical foundation and failure to specify assessment and integration procedures. An additional limitation is a lack of explicit criteria for discriminating between taxa. Although this may be due largely to a lack of concern with taxonomy, it prevents testing the reliability and validity of psychodynamic conceptions of differences between disorders.

The major limitation of current multivariate taxonomies is their reliance on a particular type of assessment data. Although structured ratings are the most common type of multivariate data, it is not ratings per se, but the derivation of taxa from a single type of data—ratings or otherwise—that constitutes a limitation. Different data may yield different taxa. Like the other two major paradigms, the multivariate paradigm faces challenges in integrating diverse data of varying reliability and validity into optimal taxonomic distinctions.

SUMMARY

The Kraepelinian taxonomic paradigm originated with the application of nineteenth-century medical nosology to adult mental disorders. It was based on the assumption that clinical descriptions could pinpoint distinctive syndromes for which organic causes would eventually be found. The *DSM*, GAP, WHO, and *ICD*-9 taxonomies of childhood disorders follow the Kraepelinian model of categorical nosology, although they do not necessarily imply an organic cause for each disorder. *DSM*-III provides more explicit criteria than the other taxonomies, but they all lack operational definitions.

Although Kraepelinian taxonomies are often called "diagnostic systems," "diagnosis" in this context refers only to "classification." *Formal diagnoses* made according to these systems do not yield *diagnostic formulations* any more than do other taxonomies.

The Kraepelinian approach facilitated the identification of disorders having clear organic features and/or patterns of clearly pathognomonic behavior. *DSM*-III returned to the ideals of Kraepelinian nosology in providing more explicit descriptive criteria for distinguishing among disorders than did *DSM*-I or *DSM*-II. The criteria for some major adult disorders were derived from research diagnostic criteria. Yet the child and adolescent categories of *DSM*-III, like those of the GAP, WHO, *ICD*-9, *DSM*-I, and *DSM*-II, are based on negotiated criteria for clinical concepts. This fact and the lower reliability of child than adult diagnoses raises the following questions: How appropriate is this approach to behaviors that many children show to some extent without discernible physical pathology? How can this approach make better use of empirical data to operationally define childhood disorders? What are the relative advantages and disadvantages of a taxonomy based on categorical clinical concepts?

The psychodynamic approach has not been much concerned with taxonomy, but psychoanalytic theory had a major impact on the definition of neurotic disorders in the *DSM*-I and GAP taxonomies and was influential in denying the possibility of childhood depression. Anna Freud's Developmental Profile provides a model for psychodynamic assessment and taxonomy, but the subordination of description to inferred psychodynamics raises the following questions: Is it possible to make reliable and valid inferences of the sort used to define disorders in terms of psychodynamic theory? How can idiographic personality formulations provide a basis for taxonomy? How can we determine the relevance of psychodynamics to less inferential definitions of disorders?

In the multivariate taxonomic paradigm, standardized assessment data are analyzed to detect covariation among groups of attributes. Although subjective judgment is involved in the selection of samples, assessment data, and analytic methods, a particular multivariate analysis aggregates a particular data set in a perfectly reliable way. This avoids the unreliability of aggregating data mentally.

Despite differences in subject samples, assessment procedures, and analytic methods, various studies have converged on a few broad-band syndromes and more numerous narrow-band syndromes. Some have counterparts in Kraepelinian taxonomies, but there is little correspondence between other multivariate and Kraepelinian syndromes.

Beside the empirical derivation of syndromes, multivariate methods such as cluster analysis can be used to construct typologies of individuals who share similar profiles. The quantitative nature of both the syndromes and profile types enables us to score the degree to which individuals manifest particular syndromes and resemble particular profile types. Multivariate taxonomy is rigorously derived from assessment data, but its dependence on particular assessment data raises the following questions: How can multivariate descriptions be linked to other relevant data, such as the age of the child and duration of the problems?

How can multivariate taxonomy integrate different types of data from different sources? How can the quantitative relations captured by multivariate methods be used to improve upon traditional categorical concepts of disorders?

The behavioral approach currently lacks a taxonomic paradigm of its own. Although some behavior modifiers acknowledge that classification is unavoidable, others reject both standardized assessment and taxonomy. Service-based taxonomies are used to specify criteria for services. Ecological approaches have been proposed to avoid stigmas associated with "labeling," but they do not offer a testable basis for assessment or taxonomy.

The major paradigms are vulnerable to the representativeness heuristic and have certain other limitations, such as a lack of operational basis for utilizing assessment data (Kraepelinian paradigm); lack of explicit criteria for discriminating between taxa (psychodynamic paradigm); and reliance on one type of assessment data (multivariate paradigm). The Kraepelinian and psychodynamic paradigms are both vulnerable to illusory correlation, inability to assess covariation, and confirmatory bias. The Kraepelinian paradigm appears to be the most vulnerable to the availability heuristic.

5

DEVELOPMENTAL AND METRICAL QUESTIONS

Chapter 1 illustrated some typical problems for which children and adolescents are referred for help. These included the following:

- A 32-month-old girl with poor language development, resistance to toilet training, and no interest in other children.
- An 8-year-old boy with reading problems, disruptive classroom behavior, fighting, and no friends.
- A 14-year-old girl having conflicts with her mother, possible marijuana use, declining school performance, crying spells, and poor eating and sleeping habits.
- A highly intelligent 18-year-old youth who seemed depressed, had become erratic in school, harbored suspicious and suicidal thoughts, and may have experimented with hallucinogenic drugs.

Questions about the cases focused on four issues:

(1) The type and degree of deviance in areas such as speech, social skills, activity level, attention, conflict with parents, school performance, delinquency, eating and sleeping, emotional states, and suicidal ideation.
(2) Constructs that might "explain" the observed problems, such as infantile autism, learning disability, emancipation conflict, identity crisis, and psychosis.
(3) The kind of help to provide.
(4) The long-term prognosis and plans to be made.

Specific etiologies would also be of great interest, but too little is known about the specific etiology of most child and adolescent disorders to help much in current assessment, taxonomy, and treatment. Although it is certainly important to seek etiologies, the many variables apt to affect most disorders make it unlikely that we will soon be able to undo specific causes. Instead, there will be a continuing need for clinical creativity in ameliorating ongoing pathogenic influences while facilitating development.

DEVELOPMENTAL QUESTIONS

The issues raised by our illustrative cases highlight the need for viewing children's disorders from developmental perspectives. The referring complaints involved a combination of behavior that was troublesome to others—such as aggression—and failure to show expected developmental progress in areas such as speech, toileting, social relations, scholastic achievement, adaptation to school culture, friendships, relations with family, and preparation for adult roles. Most childhood disorders involve deviance *relative* to norms for the child's chronological age, biological maturation, cognitive level, grade in school, and behavior of peers. A key question, therefore, is how to compare a child's functioning with that of normal children at particular developmental levels.

Some behaviors, such as 2-year-olds' resistance to toilet training and adolescents' rejection of parental values, may be severe enough to upset parents without deviating from the normal range for the child's developmental level. In such cases interventions should help parents deal with the child's normal behavior more than seeking fundamental changes in the child. When children's behavior deviates markedly from norms for their developmental level, however, we need to know the probabilities of various outcomes. Unfortunately, a lack of operational definitions for child and adolescent disorders and a paucity of good outcome studies limit the precision with which prognoses can now be stated. There are sufficient data, however, to illustrate developmental issues with respect to conduct problems, hyperactivity, and depression, as discussed next.

Conduct Disorders

The term "conduct disorder" refers to behavior that violates common standards of honesty and respect for the rights of others. Multivariate

TABLE 5.1
Aggressive and Delinquent Syndromes
Found for Children Ages 4-16

Aggressive Syndrome*	Delinquent Syndrome**
Argues a lot	Hangs around children who get
Cruelty, bullying, or meanness to others	in trouble
Demands a lot of attention	Lying or cheating
Disobedient at home	Runs away from home
Easily jealous	Steals at home
Gets in many fights	Steals outside the home
Physically attacks people	Swearing or obscene language
Screams a lot	
Stubborn, sullen, or irritable	
Sudden changes in mood or feelings	
Teases a lot	
Temper tantrums or hot temper	
Threatens people	
Unusually loud	

SOURCE: Achenbach and Edelbrock (1983).
*Items occurring together in at least four of six factor analyses of clinically referred children of each sex ages 4-5, 6-11, and 12-16.
**Items occurring together in at least four of five factor analyses for boys ages 4-5 and both sexes ages 6-11 and 12-16. (Syndrome not found for girls ages 4-5.)

studies of children's behavior problems have repeatedly identified two separate syndromes of problems corresponding to the concept of conduct disorders. One involves mainly overt aggression and conflict with others, and the other involves more covert dishonesty and rule-breaking behavior. Table 5.1 shows items common to versions of these syndromes that have been identified in separate factor analyses for each sex at ages 4-5, 6-11, and 12-16. These two syndromes are by no means mutually exclusive, as second-order analyses have shown that they both load on a broad-band factor described with labels such as "undercontrolled" and "externalizing" (see Chapter 4 for details). This means that children with features of one conduct disorder syndrome often have features of the other syndrome as well.

The terms *Aggressive* and *Delinquent* are used to summarize the content of the syndromes in Table 5.1. It should be noted, however, that the term Delinquent does not necessarily mean that a child breaks laws or is adjudicated by a court. Instead, Delinquent is used here in its generic sense of violating rules of social conduct. If the behavior of either the Aggressive or Delinquent syndrome is severe enough in later childhood and adolescence, arrest may indeed result. However, aggressive and delinquent behavior problems should not be equated with legal concepts of juvenile delinquency. Many children who show aggressive or delinquent behavior are never arrested and those who are arrested do not necessarily show either the Aggressive or Delinquent syndromes. Because we are concerned primarily with evidence on the developmental course of particular behavior problems, we will not deal with the legal aspects here. (For relations between the developmental and legal aspects, see Achenbach, 1982, chap. 13; Rutter & Giller, 1983).

In much of the literature on conduct problems, the Aggressive syndrome is called "Unsocialized Aggressive," whereas the Delinquent syndrome is called "Socialized Delinquent." This reflects assumptions that children showing the Aggressive syndrome do not have social attachments to other people, whereas those showing the Delinquent syndrome have positive social relations, albeit with delinquent peers. As shown in Table 5.1, the empirically derived Delinquent syndrome includes the item "hangs around children who get in trouble," whereas the Aggressive syndrome includes no signs of positive relations with anybody. *DSM*-III added further permutations of the socialized-unsocialized and aggressive-delinquent distinctions by dividing conduct disorder into four types (omitted from *DSM*-III-R):

(1) Undersocialized Aggressive
(2) Undersocialized Nonaggressive
(3) Socialized Aggressive
(4) Socialized Nonaggressive

Because *DSM*-III provided no overarching definition of conduct disorder, it implied that these are separate disorders to be distinguished from one another. There is, however, little evidence that either the socialized-undersocialized or aggressive-nonaggressive distinction can be made in a sufficiently categorical fashion to justify this four-fold typology. A study of *DSM*-III diagnoses, for example, showed that 52% of a heterogeneous sample of outpatient children met the criteria for at least one conduct disorder. Many of these children also met the criteria for other conduct disorders, Oppositional disorder, and Attention Deficit disorder (Costello et al., 1984). Furthermore, behavior profiles of children who are quite deviant in terms of either the Aggressive or Delinquent syndrome (Table 5.1) show a variety of deviance in other areas. Among 12-16-year-old girls, for example, one group having exceptionally high scores on the Delinquent syndrome also shows exceptional deviance in aggression and depressed withdrawal, whereas a second group is deviant only on the Delinquent syndrome (Achenbach & Edelbrock, 1983).

The salience of conduct problems, the concern they arouse, and the seriousness of their counterparts in adulthood have stimulated more long-term outcome research than have most other behavior problems of childhood. Because children's conduct problems are usually quite evident, they are easier to study than problems that are more subtle or ambiguous. They therefore make a better starting point for considering certain developmental questions than do less conspicuous problems.

Definitional Questions

More than most problems, conduct problems have clear counterparts across nearly the entire life span, from early childhood through old age. Even in infancy, persistent temper tantrums and resistance to socialization might be considered early versions of the Aggressive syndrome shown in Table 5.1. Lying, stealing, and fraternizing with bad companions obviously cannot begin until later ages, but at least some behaviors of the Delinquent syndrome are evident by the preschool period. Factor analyses have identified a syndrome among clinically referred 4-5-year-old boys that includes firesetting, vandalism, bad companions, swearing, and stealing (Achenbach & Edelbrock, 1983).

Although it is easy to identify aggressive and delinquent behaviors, it is harder to define conduct "disorders." The *DSM* criteria, for example, specify violent behaviors that are uncommon before adolescence. By then, however, it may be hard to determine which conduct problems reflect (1) a "disorder" versus (2) an aggressive or delinquent lifestyle consistent with one's subculture versus (3) a transient adolescent rebellion against authority.

These distinctions become especially questionable when aggressive and delinquent behaviors come under the purview of the law. Unlike younger ages—when conduct problems concern mainly the family, school, and helping professions—adolescents showing such behaviors are often viewed as lawbreakers, rather than as needing help for a "disorder." The need to deter, punish, and segregate potentially dangerous lawbreakers causes a radical shift in adult views of behaviors like those that evoke more therapeutic concerns at younger ages.

The impact of the child's age on adult reactions to conduct problems illustrates a developmental issue of particular importance for the definition of disorders. Despite the relative ease of ascertaining aggressive and delinquent behavior and its obviously detrimental nature, prevailing concepts of "disorders" raise different conceptual problems at different ages. Although aggressive and delinquent behavior can occur at very young ages, the inability of young children to engage in the degrees of violence and dishonesty required to meet criteria for conduct disorders argues against such diagnoses. By the ages at which the requisite behaviors become possible, nosological concepts are greatly complicated by legal questions, questions of cultural and personal lifestyle, and questions of transient developmental phenomena.

Longitudinal Course

Beside the definitional issues raised by viewing disorders cross-sectionally, the longitudinal course of conduct disorders raises a host of other developmental questions. Numerous long-term follow-up studies show that children with conduct problems often have adaptational problems in later life (e.g., Olweus, 1979; Robins, 1974; Robins, & Ratcliff, 1979; Roff & Wirt, 1984). Most of these studies, however, lacked standardized assessment of the children's initial behavior. In an influential follow-up of conduct problems, for example, Lee Robins (1974) described the clinic records from which she worked as follows:

> Unfortunately, the terms in which the clinic diagnosis was presented were seldom standard diagnostic terms . . . the terms used varied so much from year to year that it was difficult to decide how to translate them into current diagnostic categories. The more common diagnoses—personality difficulties, character difficulties, emotional immaturity—appeared in some years to be synonymous, since as one appeared the others disappeared, but in other years they appeared together, suggesting that they each represented discriminable groups of children. . . . Because most of the children fell into ill-defined and fluctuating diagnostic categories, it did not seem possible to attempt to validate the early diagnoses against the patients' adult psychiatric picture. (pp. 15-17)

> It was not possible to tell whether problems *not* appearing in a patient's record had been denied by the informant or whether the interviewer had failed to ask about them. (p. 136)

To identify specific features of early conduct problems that predict later aggressive and delinquent behavior, Loeber (1982) combined data from many studies to compare children who later showed chronic conduct problems with those who did not. He concluded that the more extreme the initial conduct problems, the more stable they were over long periods of development. The extremity of the problems was assessed in terms of four dimensions:

(1) The *density* of the problem behaviors (i.e., the initial intensity, rate, or degree of deviance involved).
(2) The *number of different settings* in which the problem behaviors occurred (i.e., home, school, neighborhood, general community).
(3) The *variety* of antisocial behaviors (i.e., the number of different types of aggressive and delinquent behaviors).
(4) The *age of onset* of antisocial behavior problems (i.e., the younger the onset, the greater the risk of chronic aggression and delinquency in later life).

Loeber found that each of the four dimensions—density, multiplicity of settings, variety, and age of onset—was associated with the long-term continuation of conduct problems in adolescence and adulthood. Although overt aggressive behavior tended to give way to more covert delinquent behavior, Loeber's analyses illustrate how quantitative assessment dimensions can detect important associations between behavior problems across extensive developmental periods.

Loeber also considered the possibility that reports of extreme deviance at one point in time would be subject to statistical regression at later points in time. That is, extreme ratings on one occasion may result partly from measurement errors and other variables that do not have exactly the same effects on a second occasion as they did on the first. Individuals who obtain extreme scores on one occasion may therefore obtain scores closer to the mean of their population on a second occasion. Loeber found, however, that children who were reported to be most deviant in conduct problems on one occasion tended to remain very deviant on subsequent occasions. There was also a tendency for children showing intermediate degrees of deviance to become more deviant. Children who initially showed no deviance, however, seldom became very aggressive or delinquent. Despite the potential for statistical regression, Loeber's findings thus seem to reflect solid and persisting characteristics of important behavior disorders.

Normative Questions

At certain points in their development, most children show at least some behaviors of the Aggressive and Delinquent syndromes. "Disobedient at home," for example, is one of the highest loading items of the Aggressive syndrome shown in Table 5.1. Yet it is common among normal children, being reported for 52% of nonreferred 4-5-year-olds, declining thereafter to about 20% of nonreferred 16-year-olds (Achenbach & Edelbrock, 1981). Another high loading item, "temper tantrums," is reported for 41% of nonreferred 4-5-year-old boys, declining to about 24% of 16-year-old boys. A potentially more serious highloading item, "cruelty, bullying, or meanness to others," is reported for about 21% of nonreferred 4-5-year-olds of both sexes, declining by the age of 16 to 14% for boys and 3% for girls. From the Delinquent syndrome shown in Table 5.1, "lying or cheating" is reported for 23% of nonreferred 4-5-year-olds, declining to 15% of 16-year-olds.

Although the occasional occurrence of mildly aggressive or delinquent behavior might be easily dismissed, many nonreferred children are reported to show a lot of the behaviors listed in Table 5.1. For example, when parents score items of the Aggressive syndrome as 0 = not true, 1 = somewhat or sometimes true, and 2 = very true or often true, the syndrome scores of nonreferred boys average 9.7 at ages 4-5, 7.3 at ages 6-11, and 5.7 at ages 12-16 (Achenbach & Edelbrock, 1983). To reach the "clinical" range of deviance on these syndromes (above the 98th percentile obtained by normative samples), 4-5-year-old boys need a score of 20, 6-11-year-old boys a score of 21, and 12-16-year-old boys a score of 22. The averages and distributions of scores obtained by girls are quite similar on their versions of these syndromes. This indicates that aggressive behavior is so common among normative groups of children that even a fairly large amount of it is not statistically deviant.

Loeber's (1982) analyses showed that several quantitative parameters of early aggressive and delinquent behavior predict severe conduct problems in later developmental periods. But how can these longitudinal statistical associations help us judge the clinical significance of a particular child's behavior? The statistical associations between early and later behavior reflect only stabilities in the rank ordering of subjects in a sample *relative* to other subjects in that particular sample. If subjects tend to retain similar ranks or categories at Time 1 and Time 2, a predictive relation is established, even though the *magnitude* of all scores may have changed greatly. To translate these statistical associations into criteria for judging the individual child, a *metric* is needed for determining whether that child is more similar to agemates who are considered normal or to those considered deviant.

Relations to Other Aspects of Development

The salience of conduct problems and the alarm they cause can divert attention from important differences among children who manifest them. Although some aggressive children alienate everyone, others are popular with peers who admire physical prowess (e.g., Milich & Landau, 1984). Similarly, some delinquent children may be adept at manipulating people. Such skills can be self-defeating, however, if they earn reinforcement for behavior that is maladaptive in the long run.

Children with conduct problems may also differ from one another in cognitive and academic skills that have a major impact on later development. An aggressive child who does not learn to read, for example, will have fewer options for adaptive development than one whose academic skills progress normally. In fact, aggressive and delinquent behavior may often be a way of camouflaging academic deficiencies. Although such deficiencies will handicap any child, other skills—such as athletic, artistic, and mechanical—should be assessed to determine if they offer alternative means for positive adaptive development.

Beside adaptive skills, it is important to assess problems that may go unnoticed when people are upset about a child's aggressive or delinquent behavior. Cluster analyses of behavior problem profiles, for example, show that some very aggressive 6-11-year-old boys are also very deviant in depression and social withdrawal (Achenbach & Edelbrock, 1983). The etiology, appropriate treatment, and developmental course of these boys' problems may differ markedly from those of boys whose deviance is restricted to aggression.

Moving now from observable behaviors to other aspects of development, biological and cognitive maturation affect problem behaviors, the contingencies supporting them, and the possibilities for treatment. Some behaviors, such as rape and murderous aggression, obviously require certain levels of biological maturation, whereas other behaviors, such as systematic burglaries, require certain cognitive attainments. Individual differences in maturational course can also affect problem behavior. Testosterone levels in boys, for example, are significantly correlated with self-reported aggression (Olweus, Mattson, Schalling, & Löw, 1980). Boys with high testosterone levels may therefore respond more aggressively to particular environmental stimuli than boys with low testosterone levels.

Just as cognitive and biological advances bring new possibilities for problem behavior, they also bring new possibilities for intervention. Therapies that emphasize cognitive strategies, moral judgment, and

TABLE 5.2
Hyperactive Syndrome Found for Children Ages 6-16*

Acts too young for his/her age
Can't concentrate, can't pay attention for long
Can't sit still, restless or hyperactive
Confused or seems to be in a fog
Daydreams or gets lost in his/her thoughts
Impulsive or acts without thinking
Poorly coordinated or clumsy
Poor school work
Prefers playing with younger children

SOURCE: Achenbach and Edelbrock (1983).
*Items occurring together in at least three of four factor analyses of clinically referred children of each sex ages 6-11 and 12-16.

social skills training, for example, are inappropriate for children who lack the levels of cognitive or social functioning required to assimilate the therapeutic inputs. Furthermore, as maturation reduces children's dependence on their families, family dynamics can take on different roles in both maintaining and changing problem behavior. During the preschool and early school years, family contingencies often play a major role in conduct problems. Changes in family members' behavior toward the child may therefore be a prerequisite for changes in the child. In later years, on the other hand, the child's behavior may have to change before family dynamics can change much.

Hyperactivity

Hyperactivity further illustrates developmental issues bearing on disruptive behavior. Second-order factor analyses show that empirically identified syndromes of hyperactivity, such as the one in Table 5.2, constitute part of the same broad-band grouping that includes the aggressive and delinquent syndromes shown in Table 5.1. As discussed earlier, this broad-band grouping has been given names such as "externalizing" and "undercontrolled." The correlations between the hyperactive, aggressive, and delinquent syndromes that are reflected in the broad-band grouping, however, do not necessarily mean that they all represent a unitary disorder. Research on boys diagnosed as hyperactive, for example, has shown that they vary along two clearly separable dimensions of hyperactivity and aggression (Langhorne & Loney, 1979; Milich, Loney, & Landau, 1982). Even though all the boys were diagnosed as hyperactive, assessment in terms of the two dimensions showed that they could be divided into four subgroups:

(1) high on hyperactivity/low on aggression
(2) high on aggression/low on hyperactivity
(3) high on both dimensions
(4) low on both dimensions

In other words, some boys clinically diagnosed as hyperactive were aggressive, but aggression was not always a concomitant of hyperactivity. Long-term follow-ups showed that high childhood scores on aggression predicted adolescent conduct problems, whereas high childhood scores on hyperactivity predicted adolescent academic problems (Loney, Kramer, & Milich, 1981). When it was present, aggression thus had different long-term correlates than did hyperactivity.

Beside differing from conduct problems in long-term correlates, hyperactivity has often been viewed as a symptom of an underlying organic abnormality. For many years, hyperactivity was virtually a synonym for minimal brain damage (MBD) and even for learning disabilities (e.g., Ochroch, 1981). When research revealed little evidence for brain damage in most hyperactive children (e.g., Brown et al., 1981), other organic causes were postulated, such as food sensitivities (Feingold, 1976) and neurotransmitter abnormalities (Wender & Wender, 1978).

"Hyperactivity" is often a general wastebasket term for nuisance behavior, especially in school. Stimulant drugs, such as Ritalin, are widely used without standardized assessment to determine whether overactivity is indeed the central problem. Children for whom such medication is prescribed have been found to avoid taking it, however, often unbeknownst to their physicians (Sleator, Ullmann, & von Neumann, 1982). Failure to take the medication may help to explain the poor functioning found in long-term follow-ups of children for whom medication was prescribed (e.g., Blouin, Bornstein, & Trites, 1978; Gittelman, 1982; Loney, Whaley-Klahn, Kosier, & Conboy, 1983).

A shift of views on hyperactivity led to the renaming of the *DSM*-II's "hyperkinetic reaction" as "attention deficit disorder with hyperactivity" in *DSM*-III (APA, 1968, 1980). As shown in Table 5.2, versions of the hyperactive syndrome identified empirically through factor analysis have typically included attentional problems, such as "can't concentrate." There is little proof, however, that either attentional problems or overactivity constitute the essential core of this syndrome. Instead, most normal children manifest at least some of the behaviors shown in Table 5.2 in some degree and in some situations at some time in their lives. These behaviors are neither intrinsically pathognomonic nor harmful.

Yet when the number of behaviors of this kind, their intensity, and/or their situational inappropriateness are excessive for a child's age, they can impede the acquisition of skills and the social relationships needed for normal development.

Our present knowledge tells us neither a specific etiology, nor an optimal treatment, nor the relative precedence of attentional deficits versus overactivity. Our primary assessment task is, therefore, not to determine whether the child "has the disorder," but to determine how deviant the child is with respect to the particular constellation of behaviors and how they jeopardize development. Evidence for developmental declines in uncontrolled activity and for developmental improvements in attention (Milich, 1984) further argues for comparing problems of attention and overactivity with normative-developmental baselines.

Depression

Aggressive and delinquent behaviors have long commanded attention because of the trouble they cause. Hyperactivity gained widespread attention largely because of its disruptiveness in school. Children's depressive problems, by contrast, are not so obvious to other people. Furthermore, the psychoanalytic theory dominant from the 1930s through the 1960s denied that true depressive disorders could occur before the superego matured in adolescence. In the late 1960s and 1970s, however, a search for childhood depression began, inspired largely by renewed interest in adult affective disorders and the apparent efficacy of antidepressant medications for adults.

In the absence of empirical criteria for childhood depression, assumptions about the biological nature of adult affective disorders were extrapolated to children. Because children seldom report depression as such, various other problems were interpreted as "depressive equivalents" or "symptoms of depressive illness." Such symptoms included abdominal pain, headaches, fears, temper tantrums, aggression, and changes in school performance (Frommer, 1967; Weinberg et al., 1973). Interpretations of depression were further broadened by the construct of "masked depression," which was inferred from aggression, hyperactivity, and other problem behaviors (Cytryn & McKnew, 1979, p. 327). This concept was later repudiated (Cytryn, McKnew, & Bunney, 1980), but confusion remains about how to define depressive disorders of childhood.

The *DSM*-III assumed that "the essential features of a major depressive episode are similar in infants, children, adolescents, and adults" (APA, 1980, p. 211). It therefore included no separate depressive disorders of childhood, but did provide slight modifications of adult criteria for diagnosing depressive episodes in children under 6. One modification was that dysphoric (unhappy) mood could be inferred from a persistently sad facial expression, rather than being reported by the child. A second modification was that three symptoms out of a subset of four from an overall list of eight symptoms had to be present, whereas any four of the eight symptoms satisfied criteria for adults. Yet there was no empirical basis for the choice of 6 years as a dividing line, for the particular modifications of the adult criteria, or for the assumption that child, adolescent, and adult depressive disorders are otherwise similar.

Children seldom complain of depression, and there has been little empirical basis for inferring childhood depression as a circumscribed disorder. It is therefore important to distinguish between signs and self-reports of depression as an *affect*, as a set of cooccurring features that constitute a *syndrome*, and as a *disorder* involving impairment.

Even though depression was seldom a reason for referral at that time, data collected from 1973 through 1977 showed that parents' reports of the item "unhappy, sad, or depressed" discriminated between clinically referred and nonreferred children more strongly than any of 117 other problem items (Achenbach & Edelbrock, 1981). The prevalence rates ranged from 43% for referred versus 3% for nonreferred 4-5-year-old boys, to 86% versus 13% for 12-13-year-old girls. Teachers' ratings also showed that the item "unhappy, sad, or depressed" was an especially powerful discriminator between referred and nonreferred school children (Edelbrock & Achenbach, 1985). It is thus apparent that depressive affect persistent enough to be noted by parents and teachers is a strong sign that all is not well with a child.

Factor analyses of parents' ratings of the 118 items used in this research have yielded a clearcut syndrome of features like those used to make clinical diagnoses of depression, as shown in Table 5.3. Like the factor-analytically derived aggressive, delinquent, and hyperactive syndromes shown in Tables 5.1 and 5.2, however, the composition of the depressed syndrome varies with the age and sex of the children. Among 12-16-year-old girls, for example, the depressive syndrome includes more items indicative of withdrawal than versions of the syndrome found for children between the ages of 4 and 11. Furthermore, the distributions of total scores on the various versions of the syndrome differ by age and sex. These age and sex variations are missed when categorical criteria for adult disorders are applied to children.

TABLE 5.3
Depressed Syndrome Found for Children Ages 4-11

Complains of loneliness
Fears he/she might think or do something bad
Feels he/she has to be perfect
Feels or complains that no one loves him/her
Feels others are out to get him/her
Feels too guilty
Feels worthless or inferior
Self-conscious or easily embarrassed
Sulks a lot
Too fearful or anxious
Unhappy, sad, or depressed
Worrying

SOURCE: Achenbach and Edelbrock (1983).
*Items occurring together in at least three of four factor analyses of clinically referred children of each sex at ages 4-5 and 6-11.

Although depressive affects and syndromes are evident in children, questions still remain as to how we should define depressive *disorders* in childhood. There is evidence that children meeting *DSM*-III criteria for depressive disorders continue having depressive episodes in adolescence. Even in these cases, however, depressive features are often accompanied by other problem behaviors (Kovacs, Feinberg, Crouse-Novak, Paulauskas, & Finkelstein, 1984; Kovacs, Feinberg, Crouse-Novak, Paulauskas, Pollock, & Finkelstein, 1984). The high prevalence rate for depressive affect in referred children and the variety of associated problems suggest multiple causal factors, such as the following:

(1) In some cases depressive affect may be a response to negative feedback from people irked by children's other problem behavior.
(2) It may reflect chldren's own distress about their other maladaptive behavior.
(3) It may be one of several responses to life stress, such as family conflict.
(4) It may indeed be symptomatic of an endogenous depressive disorder.

Like other general indices of maladaptation, such as poor school work, persistent unhappiness in a child is apt to be a sign of trouble, regardless of its specific etiology. Some depressed children may ultimately be found to have depressive disorders like those that respond to antidepressants in adults. The prevalence of depressed affect among clinically referred children, however, indicates that depressed affect deserves attention in its own right, rather than merely as a possible sign of endogenous depression. Whether or not a child has such an illness, chronic unhappiness can impede the development of social relationships and adaptive skills. By the same token, improvement in affect—like school performance—may be a good global index of improved adaptive functioning, even if depressed affect was initially a by-product rather than a cause of behavior problems.

METRICAL QUESTIONS

In considering developmental aspects of assessment and taxonomy, metrical questions arise in several forms. One concerns the need to tag problem behaviors for analysis in relation to other variables. Designating behaviors as present versus absent (scored 1 versus 0)—the most rudimentary form of metrification—may be adequate for some purposes. Even slightly greater differentiation, however, such as not true versus somewhat or sometimes true versus very true or often true (scored 0-1-2), can greatly increase precision. Precision can also be improved by combining similar or related items into scales, so that a particular problem or syndrome is measured by a sum or other aggregation of multiple data points. Because each item may tap only one aspect of a disorder and may be subject to unique sources of error, scale scores based on multiple items usually are more reliable and valid than single items.

Normative Issues

Aside from general psychometric considerations, metrical questions arise from the need to relate particular measurements to the child's developmental level. This is true for most characteristics, including physical, behavioral, social-emotional, cognitive, and academic. Knowledge of a child's height, testosterone level, frequency of temper tantrums, number of friends, or score on a test, for example, is of little use without reference to normative data for the child's age. We therefore need to determine a variable's distribution in normative samples of children at each age.

For some purposes, reference groups other than general population samples may be desired. In assessing mentally retarded children, for example, it is important to compare their behavior and achievement with that of other retarded children. Some scales for assessing the retarded do this by providing separate sets of standard scores based on "normative" samples of retarded children and of nonretarded children (e.g., the *Adaptive Behavior Scales* of the American Association on Mental Deficiency, 1981). This enables us to compare a child with other children having similar handicaps and with nonretarded agemates with whom the child may have to interact in mainstream and neighborhood environments. Whatever the reference group, however, it is helpful to view a particular child's scores in relation to those obtained by relevant groups of children. This is true even for observational measures, in which observation of several control children can provide "local norms" with which to compare a target child's behavior in the same situation (Achenbach & Edelbrock, 1983; Reed & Edelbrock, 1983; Walker & Hops, 1976).

Developmental Versus Trait Variance

Because many attributes of children are correlated with development, a correlation between two measures may reflect the variance that both share with development, rather than a separate, enduring feature of the children. As an example, impulsivity has been viewed as a cognitive style trait underlying learning problems, hyperactivity, aggression, and delinquency. Numerous studies report correlations between behavior problems and measures of impulsivity, such as the Matching Familiar Figures test, which requires subjects to pick the member of a multiple choice array that matches a standard figure (see Cairns & Cammock, 1978). It has also been found, however, that measures of impulsivity correlate with indices of development, such as chronological age and mental age (MA).

To determine whether measures of impulsivity tap a trait that is independent of development, Achenbach and Weisz (1975) assessed children's impulsivity with a version of the Matching Familiar Figures test on two occasions, six months apart. A significant correlation between Time 1 and Time 2 impulsivity scores suggested that they reflected a stable trait. It was found, however, that initial MA on the Stanford-Binet accounted for considerably more variance in Time 2 impulsivity than did Time 1 impulsivity. Furthermore, a significant negative correlation between impulsivity and hypothesis usage on learning tasks disappeared when MA was partialled out. In other words, the apparent stability of impulsivity over the six-month interval and its negative association with hypothesis usage largely reflected the developmental variance tapped by Stanford-Binet MA. A similar lack of independence from general cognitive development has been found for measures of another cognitive style, field independence (Weisz, O'Neill, & O'Neill, 1975), and moral development (Taylor & Achenbach, 1975).

Beside psychometrically assessed "traits," childhood attributes assessed in other ways correlate with general indices of development. Perceptual-motor performance on the Bender Gestalt figure copying test, for example, has been found to correlate .85 with MA (Koppitz, 1975). Although marked deviation from norms for a child's mental age may indicate a specific perceptual-motor problem, much of the variance in the quality of drawings thus overlaps with cognitive development.

Assessments of children's neurological functioning have also been found to correlate with indices of development. A standardized neurological examination for children, the Physical and Neurological Examination for Soft Signs (PANESS), for example, has been described as a "developmental scale," because signs of deviance correlated .66 with age (Mikkelsen, Brown, Minichiello, Millican, & Rapoport, 1982). A correlation also found with IQ suggests that the correlation with MA would have been still larger than with chronological age. Similarly, performance on the Halstead-Reitan neuropsychological test battery correlates significantly with cognitive levels in children (Seidenberg, Giordani, Berent, & Boll, 1983).

The likely associations between developmental changes and most forms of deviance argue for calibrating all assessment procedures with relevant indices of development. Different indices of development are relevant for different purposes. Indices of cognitive development, such as MA, for example, are especially relevant to assessment of functions involving cognitive and perceptual-motor maturation. If measures of a purported trait or type of deviance retain no significant stability over time after cognitive developmental variance has been partialled out, they cannot be claimed to measure any stable variables beside general cognitive development. In such cases we need to change the measure, redefine the target construct, or recognize that the construct may not be viable.

Measures of physical parameters, such as hormones, neurotransmitters, and neurological functioning, should be calibrated with general physical maturation. Although there is no single omnibus index of physical maturation, some, such as bone age, may be good approximations. These can be supplemented with others pertinent to particular types of assessment during particular developmental periods, such as standardized indices of pubertal development.

For behavioral assessment of children who are within the normal range with respect to cognitive and physical development, chronological age may be an adequate omnibus index, although variables such as socioeconomic level and ethnic background may add precision to developmental norms. Sex differences in developmental course make it desirable to have separate developmental calibrations for boys and girls.

Reliability and Stability

To be useful and valid, assessment procedures must be *reliable*. That is, a procedure must produce findings that do not change unless the target phenomena change. Although high reliability does not guarantee validity, unreliability limits the validity with which the target phenomena can be gauged. This does not necessarily mean that high reliability should be an exclusive goal, because simplifying assessment to maximize reliability can reach a point of triviality. Different goals may require different types of reliability and different ways of achieving it.

Where direct observations are used to determine whether a specific behavior occurs during a particular interval, *interobserver reliability* is important. On the other hand, where the target phenomena are assumed to be persisting characteristics that are not assessable by two observers during a limited interval, *test-retest reliability* may be more important. For multi-item tests or inventories, the intercorrelation among all the test items (*split-half reliability* or *internal consistency*) may be important. Although internal consistency coefficients are sometimes cited as evidence for the intrinsic reliability of measures, such coefficients mainly indicate the degree to which all the items tap a single variable. Some measures with high internal consistency may have low test-retest reliability or low validity, because they do not sample enough different facets of the target phenomenon.

Whereas reliability refers to the consistency of assessment procedures over periods too short for the target phenomena to change, *stability* refers to long-term consistencies in the target phenomena themselves. For most behavioral variables, test-retest reliability is judged in terms of consistencies of findings over periods ranging from hours to weeks, if no interventions take place to change the behavior. Consistent results over longer periods suggest stability in the target behavior, as well as in the assessment procedures. Like high reliability, however, high assessment stability may sometimes be gained at the cost of trivializing assessment procedures. If assessment focuses only on features that are impervious to change, for example, it cannot detect worsening or improvement in a child's condition. It is therefore important for assessment procedures to be capable of detecting changes that actually occur.

As discussed earlier, efforts to identify traits should control for developmental variance that inflates correlations between trait measures when subjects differ in developmental level. When children are studied longitudinally, developmental variance may reduce the apparent stability of certain variables, because of changes in range of variation, changes in phenotypic manifestations of the variables, or changes in children's rank order within the samples studied. When we assess either stability or reliability, we should therefore consider consistencies both in the *magnitude* of the scores being compared and in children's *rank order* within a sample.

Although Pearson correlations are often reported as reliability coefficients, they reflect mainly the similarity between the rank orders of two sets of scores, regardless of their magnitudes. As an example, subjects' scores on two occasions may be correlated +1.00, even though each subject's score declines 10 points from Time 1 to Time 2. On the other hand, tests of the differences between the magnitudes of two sets of scores, such as the t test, may show no significant difference, even though a Pearson correlation of -1.00 reveals that the subjects who scored highest at Time 1 score lowest at Time 2. The correlation of +1.00 suggests perfect reliability, whereas the correlation of -1.00 suggests no reliability. However, the changes in the magnitudes of scores present the opposite picture. Percentages of agreement between two sets of scores can also be unduly inflated by chance agreements that occur when many subjects have the same scores. This is especially likely with measures on which most subjects obtain the same score. When a particular score is very common, the probability is high that many subjects will receive that score by chance on both assessment occasions.

For quantitative data, intraclass correlations reflect agreement based on both the magnitude and rank ordering of scores. For categorical data, the statistic kappa indicates agreement after correction for chance agreements (Cohen, 1960; Fleiss, Nee, & Landis, 1979). Yet because intraclass correlations and kappa provide complex summaries of agreement, they sometimes obscure aspects of agreement and disagreement that are illuminating when viewed separately. Thus, for example, the intraclass correlation will be low if two sets of scores differ greatly in magnitude, even if the subjects have identical rank orders in the two sets of scores. This could happen over a developmental period when a particular type of behavior declines but does so uniformly for all subjects. In this case it would be preferable to compute both a test of the difference in magnitudes and a Pearson correlation coefficient. Similarly, high agreement between two sets of categorical judgments will yield a low kappa if one category has an exceptionally high base rate. It may be important to show, however, that—despite the possible contribution of chance—the actual agreement is high. This can be done by reporting the percentage of agreement or the ratio of the obtained kappa to the maximum possible, given the observed frequencies with which the available categories were used (kappa/kappa max). When all disagreements receive the same weight, measures of the reliability of categorical judgments are less informative than measures of the reliability of quantitative judgments that reflect degrees of agreement. Some variation in the "degree" of categorical agreement can be detected by using "weighted kappa," which distinguishes between more and less serious disagreements (Cohen, 1968).

Aggregation of Data to Improve
Reliability, Stability, and Validity

Any single observation or test item is vulnerable to biases and errors that limit its representativeness as a sample of a person's functioning. By combining multiple assessments of a target variable, errors of measurement can be averaged out (Rushton, Brainerd, & Pressley, 1983). In standard psychometric practice, therefore, items are summed or otherwise aggregated to provide a score. The reliability of measurement usually improves as the number of items increases.

Behavioral assessors initially eschewed psychometric considerations on the grounds that they were directly assessing the problem behavior rather than drawing inferences from indirect measures. It has become clear, however, that direct observations of behavior, like individual test items, are vulnerable to problems of unrepresentativeness arising from specificity of content, occasions, observers, and situations. To reduce these problems, observational assessment often employs time sampling to accumulate a record of the target behaviors across a series of brief intervals, such as 15 seconds. Data from the intervals are then summed to provide a score for a particular occasion. To provide more representative samples of behavior, time sampling may be repeated on several occasions. To acquire fully representative samples, however, it is also necessary to observe a variety of behavior across various situations.

Items or observations are aggregated because no single item or observation provides a perfectly reliable or representative sample of an individual's functioning. By broadening the sample of behaviors, aggregation of diverse items and observations can improve not only reliability, but the validity with which more complex constructs, such as intelligence and aggression, are assessed. Furthermore, it has been shown that aggregation of data points across many occasions can increase the reliability, stability, and validity of assessment for traits and developmental variables that are otherwise hard to substantiate (Epstein, 1983; Rushton et al., 1983). This finding has become entangled with the debate about the cross-situational consistency versus specificity of human behavior (Mischel & Peake, 1982). No matter what position one takes in the debate, however, it seems obvious that human variability necessitates aggregation of data in order to obtain reliable, stable, and valid assessment of almost anything related to psychopathology. This raises the following questions, to be discussed next:

(1) What should be aggregated?
(2) How long a period should aggregation span?
(3) How should aggregated data be summarized?

What Should Be Aggregated?

For narrowly defined observable problems, such as tics, direct observations via time sampling on a few occasions can provide an index of the rate at which the target behavior occurs. Even with target behaviors as molecular as tics, however, the rate of the behavior may vary greatly with the circumstances. The presence of the observer and the conditions under which observations are feasible may both have effects that make the obtained data unrepresentative.

If the child is sufficiently competent and motivated, an alternative is to have him or her keep a record of the tics as they occur over several days. If this is not feasible, parents or teachers can often provide nearly as complete a record. The impracticality of using direct assessment such as time sampling by trained observers and the unfeasibility of obtaining truly representative observations often necessitate reliance on reports by others, such as parents, teachers, and children themselves. For molecular problem behaviors such as tics, bedwetting, and encopresis, considerable precision can be obtained by having the informant record the number of times the behavior occurs within selected intervals. For tics, the intervals might be defined in terms of particular activities, such as eating meals, doing homework, watching television, and free play at home, or seat work, group work, and recess at school. For bedwetting and encopresis, the number of times per week would be more appropriate.

For problems that are less narrowly defined—such as aggression, fearfulness, depression, inattentiveness, and withdrawal—aggregation involves not just counting a single target behavior, but identifying classes of related behaviors. Such classes may be constructed on the basis of theory, clinical judgments of the types of problems thought to cooccur, or multivariate methods, such as factor analysis. What distinguishes item groupings of this sort from more molecular problems is that they constitute *syndromes* or sets of covarying features that together define the problem. Empirically derived aggressive, delinquent, hyperactive, and depressed syndromes (Tables 5.1, 5.2, and 5.3) illustrate the variety of phenotypic features that may covary. Because many of the constituent features are not scorable as discrete behavioral events, aggregation involves combining ratings or other types of scores for the density, intensity, or seriousness of all the features.

In summary, what is aggregated depends on the type of problem in question. If the problem is a molecular, easily recorded behavior, aggregation may involve merely summing or averaging the behavior's occurrence over particular intervals. Even with behaviors of this sort, however, it usually is necessary to aggregate scores over a variety of conditions, as reported by informants other than trained observers. For broader categories or syndromes, it is necessary to identify features that covary and to aggregate these covarying features, using scores for the density, variety, intensity, or seriousness of each feature. Aggregation of these scores across the covarying features usually improves the reliability, stability, and validity of assessment.

How Long a Period Should Aggregation Span?

Because behavior assessed at one moment seldom provides a representative sample, it is necessary to consider the time or occasions that assessment should span. Abilities, for example, are relatively stable, and standardized ability tests are quite reliable. Most abilities can therefore be adequately sampled by administering multiple items during a single testing session. Assessment of motivation and other variables affecting the use of abilities, however, requires sampling across occasions and situations, such as classroom versus one-to-one situations.

For easily observed problem behaviors of high frequency, assessment may need to span only a few weeks to provide a stable baseline. For problems that require more inference, are of low frequency, or comprise syndromes of covarying features, however, longer spans are needed to provide reliable and valid baselines. Because assessment of such problems depends heavily on data obtained from informants, the time intervals cannot be specified so precisely as when direct behavioral assessment is feasible. Furthermore, problems such as withdrawal and depression require judgments of a child's demeanor over substantial periods, ranging from days to months. Although such judgments are not objective records of behavioral events, they are often crucial in determining what, if anything, should be done to help the child.

How Should Aggregated Data Be Summarized?

Whether we record behavioral events as they occur within precisely defined intervals or obtain ratings of multiple features of a syndrome, we need concise summaries of the data for integration with other types of data about the child. Reports that a child on a single occasion wets the bed, hits another child, or looks unhappy are of limited use by themselves. By aggregating data over occasions or over a group of covarying features, we can obtain summary scores for the behavior. The scores have little intrinsic meaning, however, without reference to norms and / or cutoff points for distinguishing between acceptable and problem levels of the behavior. We therefore need to summarize the scores in a way that relates the child's standing to that of peers and to previously established correlates of the scores.

Standard scores based on a normative metric for a child's age are useful for indicating the *degree to which* a child's functioning is perceived as deviant from that of agemates. In addition, however, particular points or ranges on the metric must be specified as a basis for decision making. Comparison of the scores of clinically referred and "healthy" agemates, for example, can identify a cutoff point or range of scores that discriminates between the referred and healthy children. Knowledge of whether a child's score is like that of referred or healthy children can aid in deciding whether to intervene. If intervention is indicated, the choice of intervention can be based on previous findings of efficacy with children having particular scores.

It is thus important to have standardized metrics with which to summarize the status of individuals in relation to the types of decisions that assessment is expected to aid. Standardized metrics for physical variables such as temperature, pressure, weight, velocity, and distance have been crucial to the advancement of the physical sciences. Standardized metrics are mainstays of medical assessment, as exemplified by fever thermometers, blood pressure gauges, and white blood cell counts. Ability and achievement tests employ standardized metrics to compare children with agemates and to mark ranges of functioning appropriate for different services, such as those for gifted, learning disabled, and retarded children. Chapter 6 will address the application of metrical procedures to psychopathology.

IMPLICATIONS FOR COGNITIVE ECONOMICS

In previous chapters we considered the effects of human information-processing biases on various approaches to assessment and taxonomy. In this chapter we have raised developmental and metrical questions pertinent to assessment and taxonomy. We now need to consider the implications of these questions for the way we draw conclusions about children.

Two aspects of prevailing approaches to assessment and taxonomy are especially vulnerable to information-processing problems raised by developmental and metrical questions. One is the tendency to view childhood disorders as early versions of adult disorders. The other is the verbal definition of disorders in terms of categorical types.

Assumptions Based on Adult Psychopathology

Recent interest in childhood depression illustrates the tendency to base assumptions about childhood disorders on adult psychopathology. To identify early antecedents of adult depression, it undoubtedly makes sense to look for childhood counterparts. Rather than determining the range of variation and the cooccurrence of depressive features in children of various ages, however, the dominant approach was to interpret a wide range of behaviors as symptoms of depression (e.g., Cytryn & McKnew, 1979; Frommer, 1967; Weinberg et al., 1973). Because operational criteria were not specified for determining when particular behaviors were symptoms of depression, or for the density, variety, or cross-situational consistency of symptoms required to diagnose depression, inferences about childhood depression had no empirical basis. Furthermore, different criteria for childhood depression disagreed in their classification of children as depressed (Carlson & Cantwell, 1982). A burgeoning literature on childhood depression nevertheless fostered unsupported conclusions about childhood counterparts of adult depressive disorders.

Prior to the quest for childhood depression, assumptions about the childhood roots of adult schizophrenia had likewise fostered conclusions that "schizophrenogenic mothers" caused schizophrenia. Such assumptions also spawned the appellation "schizoid personality" for introverted children assumed to be future schizophrenics and the diagnosis of a variety of severely disturbed children as childhood schizophrenics. Longitudinal research has shown, however, that neither "schizophrenogenic mothers" nor childhood introversion nor "childhood schizophrenia" are common precursors of adult schizophrenia (see Achenbach, 1982, chap. 12). Studies of children at statistically high risk for adult schizophrenia because they have schizophrenic parents show, instead, that the precursors are subtle and are not evident as miniature versions of adult schizophrenia (Achenbach, 1982).

Both psychoanalysis and learning theory have long stressed the causal role of early experience in adult psychopathology. By extrapolating backward from adult disorders to childhood, these theories molded views of childhood disorders without much empirical support. In the process of molding views of childhood disorders, they also helped to shape child mental health services in the image of adult services.

Although lessons can be learned from adult disorders, excessive reliance on assumptions drawn from adult psychopathology may distort judgments of child psychopathology via several of the information-processing biases outlined in Chapter 1. If we assume that childhood disorders are early versions of adult disorders but lack developmentally appropriate operational criteria, we risk the following sources of bias:

(1) *Illusory correlation*—the tendency to incorrectly infer that attributes forming syndromes in adults also cooccur in children.
(2) *The representativeness heuristic*—the tendency to view a particular problem, such as unhappiness, as representative of or "explained by" a disorder such as depression found in adults, even though the problem may have other meanings in children.
(3) *The availability heuristic*—the tendency to categorize children in terms of salient adult diagnostic categories because it is assumed that childhood disorders are early versions of particular adult disorders and because we lack appropriate alternatives to adult categories.

(4) *The confirmatory bias*—excessive weighting of evidence consistent with assumptions that adult type disorders either cause children's behavior or are incipient in the children's current problems.

Verbal Definitions of Categorical Types

Nosologies such as the *DSM*, GAP, WHO, and *ICD*-9 systems use verbal descriptions or verbally stated rules to define disorders. They do not specify standardized operations for determining whether a child has a disorder and, if so, which disorder it is. The difficulties inherent in purely verbal formulations are evident in the differing terminology from one nosology to another and from one edition of the *DSM* to another. Difficulties also arise from the arbitrary decisions required to judge whether specific criteria are met on a yes/no basis and the arbitrary cutoff points for the number of descriptive features required to qualify for a diagnosis. Purely verbal definitions, furthermore, fail to reflect degrees of a disorder or changes in its severity over time or after treatment.

Despite the *DSM*-III efforts to make diagnostic rules more explicit, the continuing lack of operational criteria perpetuates a diagnostic process that is unduly subjective, existing above and apart from specific assessment operations. Verbal definitions that lack standardized assessment operations are vulnerable to biases of the following sort:

(1) *Illusory correlations* between features defined by fiat to be mutually associated.
(2) The *representativeness heuristic*, whereby a child's problems are thought to be "explained by" a particular verbally defined disorder even though the problems may have other causes.
(3) The *availability heuristic*, whereby the semantic matrix of verbally defined disorders shapes our interpretations of the disorders we see, and case illustrations of verbally defined categories spawn mental patterns to which new cases are matched.
(4) The *confirmatory bias*, whereby we attend mainly to evidence consistent with a particular verbally defined category.
(5) *Premature closure,* which short-circuits creative thinking when a case seems to match a verbally defined category, even though we lack operational criteria for such matching.

These problems are not apt to be solved by renegotiating the criteria for verbally defined categories or by improving the reliability with which they are used. Instead, taxonomies of child and adolescent disorders must make better use of normative-developmental data and metrical procedures.

SUMMARY

Questions about children's disorders often focus on issues such as the type and degree of deviance involved; constructs that might "explain" the observed problems; the kind of help needed; and the long-term prognosis and plans to be made. These issues highlight the need for viewing the assessment and taxonomy of children's disorders from developmental perspectives.

Research on conduct disorders, hyperactivity, and depression demonstrates the need to define disorders in relation to the range of variation found in children of particular developmental levels and to determine what features predict different long-term outcomes following intervention or nonintervention. Some problem behaviors may deserve attention in their own right at a particular developmental period without necessarily being symptomatic of an underlying or persisting disorder. Others may be important largely for their long-term significance. Furthermore, the need for help may depend more on the age of onset, density, intensity, variety, or cross-situational generality of problem behaviors than inferences about the intrinsic significance of any particular behavior.

The developmental aspects of assessment and taxonomy raise metrical issues such as the following: how to tag problem behaviors so they can be analyzed in relation to other variables; how to relate assessment to the child's developmental level; how to separate developmental variance from trait variance; and how to aggregate data to improve reliability, stability, and validity of assessment and to summarize findings.

In light of developmental and metrical questions, two aspects of prevailing approaches to assessment and taxonomy are especially vulnerable to information-processing biases: (1) the views of childhood disorders as early versions of adult disorders and (2) the verbal definitions of disorders in terms of categorical types. Both are vulnerable to illusory correlation, the representativeness heuristic, the availability heuristic, and the confirmatory bias. Verbal definitions of disorders also invite premature closure when cases seem to match categorical types despite a lack of operational criteria for determining the degree of match.

6

TAXONIC INTEGRATION OF ASSESSMENT DATA

Previous chapters have illustrated the following points:

(1) The human mind is subject to biases in:
  (a) detecting discriminative features of individuals from which to infer correlations, syndromes, and types;
  (b) combining different kinds of data to make predictions and decisions about individuals.
(2) Different assessment methods, situations, and sources of data are subject to different biases.
(3) Most taxonomies do not systematically integrate diverse assessment data.
(4) Different taxonomic paradigms are subject to different information-processing biases.
(5) Assessment and taxonomy need to take account of developmental and metrical questions.

In this chapter we will consider prospects for improving the taxonic integration of assessment data in order to facilitate research on etiology, treatment, and prognosis, as well as to aid individual children and their families. We will start by reexamining the nature and role of taxonomy.

CLASSIFICATION AND TAXONOMY

Classification refers to any systematic ordering of phenomena into groups or types. Many classification systems are constructed merely for

151

the convenience of users, without regard to intrinsic characteristics of the phenomena classified. A clinic, for example, may assign cases to therapists who have therapy hours when the cases are referred. Thereafter, the clinic may classify each case according to the child's therapist. This system may be convenient for billing, record keeping, and assignment of clinical responsibilities, but it does not reflect intrinsic differences among the cases.

Taxonomies, by contrast, are classifications that are intended to reflect intrinsic differences between cases assigned to different classes. Taxonomies of plants and animals, for example, are intended to mark important differences between groupings, such as species. Taxonomic groupings can be constructed according to a variety of criteria, including physical features, interbreeding, or hypothesized evolutionary relations. Yet even such familiar taxonomic concepts as species are mental abstractions or constructs imposed on multiple dimensions of features (Levin, 1979).

In medical taxonomies (*nosologies*), some conditions are classified according to their specific etiologies. Other conditions, however, are classified according to descriptive features if the etiology is unknown or if causal factors are less important than description of the phenotypic abnormality, as is true for most bone fractures.

Like medical nosologies, taxonomies of psychopathology employ multiple principles. Etiological criteria are employed for disorders having known etiologies, but other criteria also contribute to the classification of these disorders. In some cases of mental retardation, for example, the etiology is known to be brain damage, but an IQ test is needed to determine whether the child is functioning in the retarded range. For certain disorders, such as infantile autism, neither specific etiology nor an operational measure such as the IQ test provides definitive criteria. Yet a combination of developmental history, cognitive measures, and behavioral observations provides descriptive criteria for discriminating a class of children who seem inherently different from most other children. Although the discrimination between autistic and nonautistic children is not completely reliable and we do not know what causes the differences in the criterial features, the classification of autistic versus nonautistic is "taxonomic" in that it is based on discernible differences between the two groups.

In summary, taxonomies are put to a variety of uses, but they all aim to mark important similarities and differences between cases. For complex phenomena such as psychopathology, taxonomies embody hypothetical constructs that abstract a few of the many features characterizing individual cases. Because individual cases can differ in so many ways, choices have to be made about which features we should abstract to serve as taxonomic criteria.

Where specific etiologies are unknown, descriptive features are typically sought in hope of marking possible differences in etiology, prognosis, or need for particular treatments. To be useful, the descriptive features should at least distinguish cases according to the types of management problems they present, such as suicidal versus assaultive behavior. Once criterial features are chosen, the types or categories they define serve as hypothetical constructs to which individual cases are matched. When we abstract a few features from the many that characterize a case, we also form a hypothetical construct of the case—a conceptual abstraction intended to capture important features of the case that link it to similar cases. This raises the following question: How should we match our hypothetical constructs of individual cases to the hypothetical constructs provided by a taxonomy? Answers to this question must take account of both the methodological possibilities for assessing individual cases and the cognitive economics of matching individual features to taxonomic constructs.

PROTOTYPES AS A BASIS FOR TAXONOMY

In earlier chapters we saw the difficulties of capturing child and adolescent problems via verbally defined categories requiring yes or no decisions about each disorder. Categories of this sort are defined by criteria that are "singly necessary and jointly sufficient" for classification of individual cases (Cantor, Smith, French, & Mezzich, 1980, p. 182). Cognitive research indicates, however, that human information processing does not conform to this classical model of category usage. Even with everyday categories such as furniture, for example, the items that people categorize together do not all share a specific set of necessary and sufficient defining features (Rosch & Mervis, 1975). Instead, the items that people judge most typical of a category (e.g., table, chair) share certain features lacked by less typical items (e.g., lamp, rug). The more typical an item is of a category, the more quickly and reliably it can be categorized by most people (Smith, 1978). It thus appears that our use of categories is based on sets of imperfectly correlated features. Cases having the most features of a category are considered the most typical of the category.

The sets of imperfectly correlated features that underlie categorical judgments are known as *prototypes* (Rosch, 1978). Category membership can be computed in terms of the degree of overlap between the features of a case and the list of prototypic features that define a category. The most prototypical cases are those having the most features of a category. According to the prototype view, there is thus a quantitative basis for categorical judgments: Assignment of a case to a category depends on the number of the category's features manifested by the case.

Prototype Analyses of Diagnostic Thinking

Prototype concepts have been applied to diagnostic thinking in several ways. One approach has been to reconceptualize diagnostic judgments as prototype categorization, rather than as classical categorization based on necessary and sufficient criteria. As an example, thirteen clinicians were asked to list clinical features characterizing the prototypical patients for each of nine diagnostic categories, such as schizophenia (Cantor et al., 1980). In all nine categories, many features were listed by only one clinician, a smaller number were listed by two to four clinicians, and very few were listed by most of the clinicians. The different degrees of agreement for different features suggested that the clinicians' mental categories were described better by clusters of imperfectly correlated features than by necessary and sufficient defining criteria shared by all clinicians.

Cantor et al. analyzed features ascribed to a hierarchy of categories ranging from specific diagnoses—such as "paranoid schizophrenia"—to more general categories—such as "schizophrenia"—and still more general groupings—such as "functional psychoses." It was found that not all features of a general category were ascribed to the more specific categories nested beneath it. This "imperfect nesting" of features from one level to another is more consistent with the prototype concept of categories defined by imperfectly correlated features than with the classical concept of categories defined by necessary and sufficient criteria that are perfectly nested from one level of the hierarchy to the next.

Cantor also had clinicians make diagnoses from the case histories of patients who had eight to thirteen features of diagnostic prototypes, five to eight features, or only four features. The interclinician reliability of diagnoses was found to be significantly worse for the patients having only four prototypal features than for those having more features. The authors concluded that psychiatric diagnosis can be studied by analogy to classifications of common objects and that

> the prototype view in the psychiatric domain can allow us to use clinical training and procedures that capitalize on the orderly and principled characteristics of a prototype system, rather than expend energy trying to shape the diagnostic system to fit an idealized classical model. (Cantor et al., 1980, p. 192)

Conceptual Prototypes of Severe Childhood Disorders

In a study of prototypes of childhood disorders, experienced staff members of a residential treatment program were asked to list the most common types of disturbed children (Horowitz, Wright, Lowenstein, & Parad, 1981). The three most common labels were the "aggressive-impulsive" child, the "depressed-withdrawn" child, and the "borderline-disorganized" child. The staff then were asked to list the most usual feelings, thoughts, and behaviors of each type of child. Prototypes were formed from features that were listed with a probability of at least .29 for a type of child.

Several features met the criteria for more than one prototype. The prototype of the aggressive-impulsive child included sixteen unique features and nine features shared with the other prototypes; the prototype of the depressed-withdrawn child included eighteen unique and six shared features; and the prototype of the borderline-disorganized child included nine unique and twelve shared features, indicating considerable overlap with the other types.

Prototypes were also derived from features listed by college student staff members who were returning after one previous summer of experience in the residential treatment program ("returnees") and a second group with no previous experience ("novices"). The prototypes generated by returnees shared somewhat more features with those generated by regular staff than did the prototypes generated by the novices. Furthermore, the novices' prototypes included features not included in the prototypes generated by the more experienced groups. For example, 42% of the novices indicated that the aggressive-impulsive child feels unloved, which was not a feature of the more experienced group's prototypes. As the authors point out, if such features reflect an invalid theory of the child, the novices' treatment efforts may be antitherapeutic. The same could be true of experienced staff, however. Even though experienced staff members share certain prototypes, there is no evidence that these prototypes validly represent the children they treat.

Conceptual Prototypes of Depression

In an application of prototype analysis to concepts of depression, clinicians filled out checklists of features observed in videotaped interviews of patients (Horowitz, Post, French, Wallis, & Siegelman, 1981). Embedded in the checklists were 37 features of a prototype of depression. The clinicians also made global ratings of depression on a 5-point scale ranging from "not depressed" to "very depressed." It was found that the number of prototypic depressive features recorded on the checklist correlated .90 with the clinicians' global ratings of depression. This is consistent with findings that global ratings of other qualities covary with the number of prototypic features. Ratings of how birdlike a creature is, for example, correlate with the number of prototypic features of birds the creature has (Rosch, Mervis, Gray, Johnson, & Boyes-Graem, 1976).

Interclinician agreement for global ratings of depression was much lower for patients who did not explicitly report depression than for those who did. Disagreements in rating patients who did not report depression showed a bimodal pattern, because some clinicians judged them as slightly depressed, whereas others judged them as quite depressed (scores of 2 versus 4 on a 5-point scale). This suggests that cases with few prototypic features activate a full mental prototype of depression in some clinicians but not in others. In effect, some clinicians infer the presence of a categorical disorder in an all-or-none fashion from a few features, whereas other clinicians do not. Furthermore, when cases have only a few prototypic features, there are more possible combinations of features than when they have many features of a prototype. Both the heterogeneity of cases having few features and clinicians' differential responses to subsets of prototypic features increase information-processing biases in cases that do not closely match mental prototypes.

Theoretically, cases having features from multiple prototypes should be especially difficult to categorize. Horowitz et al. found, however, that consistency among clinicians in applying a particular diagnostic category covaried with the proportion of that category's prototypic features manifested by each case, but not with the proportion of features that were not prototypic of that category. In other words, the clinicians seemed to focus mainly on features consistent with the most salient category, while being unaffected by features associated with other categories. This reflects the confirmatory bias described in Chapter 1, whereby people attend mainly to evidence consistent with their hypotheses (Arkes & Harkness, 1983). It suggests that the confirmatory bias affects diagnostic judgments by channeling attention toward one set of prototypic features at a time.

Relations Between Diagnoses and Criterial Features

The preceding studies applied prototype analyses to clinicians' concepts of diagnostic categories. To move prototype analyses closer to the actual covariation among clinical variables, cases receiving *DSM*-III Axis II diagnoses of Borderline Personality Disorder were studied by Clarkin, Widiger, Frances, Hurt, and Gilmore (1983). Because prototypic features are not all perfectly correlated with one another or with category membership, the features are apt to differ in the diagnostic efficiency with which they indicate true members of a category. Not only may features differ in diagnostic efficiency, but a feature that has low efficiency when considered alone may gain efficiency when it occurs with certain other features. A headache alone, for example, is far less diagnostic than a headache accompanied by symptoms such as sudden sensory impairment and loss of coordination, which together suggest a cerebral hemorrhage.

DSM-III listed eight descriptive criteria for Borderline Personality Disorder, of which at least five were required to make the diagnosis. Five or more out of eight features yield 93 possible combinations, which are likely to differ in their "hit rates" for identifying true positive cases of borderline personality. Because *DSM*-III had no empirical basis for its choice of defining features or for the decision to allow any combination of five out of eight to meet criterion, Clarkin et al. tested the association of each feature with diagnoses of borderline versus other personality disorders. They did this by conducting standardized interviews in which raters judged the presence or absence of each feature of borderline personality specified by *DSM*-III.

Patients were diagnosed as having borderline personality when a majority of raters scored them as having at least five of the eight features specified by *DSM*-III. Three features were very common, being present for at least 90% of the patients diagnosed as borderline, whereas one feature was present for only 25%. There was also considerable variation in the proportion of features present, as 10% of the patients had all eight,

25% had seven, 40% had six, and 25% had five. Not only did diagnosed patients thus differ in prototypicality, but there were also differences in the combinations of features meeting the criterion.

Clarkin et al. computed conditional probabilities for the presence of a feature in borderline versus other personality disorder cases (conditional probability = the percentage of all cases manifesting the feature who also met the criterion for borderline personality). One criterial feature, "intolerance of being alone," was present in fewer cases diagnosed as borderline than receiving other diagnoses. Because only 38% of the cases having the feature met the criterion for borderline personality, its conditional probability was .38. Five other features had conditional probabilities ranging from .50 to .59, and two had conditional probabilities in the .60s. The diagnostic efficiency of each criterial feature was thus low.

By manipulating the number of features required for diagnosis, the diagnostic efficiency of the features could be changed. When the criterion was reduced from five to four out of eight features, for example, more cases were diagnosed as borderline, and the diagnostic efficiency of intolerance of being alone rose from .38 to .77. When the criterion was raised to six out of eight features, by contrast, the diagnostic efficiency of individual features fell. These changes in diagnostic efficiency partly reflect changes in the percentage of cases qualifying for the diagnosis. The diagnostic efficiency of criterial attributes typically increases as the proportion of features required for diagnosis decreases and more cases qualify for the diagnosis. Furthermore, the diagnostic efficiency of *pairs* of criterial features is higher than the features taken alone. As Clarkin et al. found, the conditional probability for the combination of identity disturbance and unstable/intense relationships was 1.0. Even combinations having this high a conditional probability, however, do not constitute necessary features for the diagnosis, as only 60% of cases diagnosed as borderline manifested both features.

Clarkin's findings go beyond prototype analyses of diagnostic thinking in that they demonstrate mismatches between nonempirically based categories, such as the *DSM*-III definition of borderline personality, and the "empirical prevalence and covariation of diagnostic features" (Clarkin et al., 1983, p. 274). Similar problems have been demonstrated in a priori classifications of behavior assessed via direct observations (Stouthamer-Loeber & Peters, 1984). This raises the question of how to improve the match between taxonomic constructs and the actual phenomena they are intended to capture, to which we now turn.

EMPIRICAL DERIVATION OF PROTOTYPES

In Chapter 4 we discussed the use of multivariate statistics to detect covariation among attributes relevant to child and adolescent psychopathology. Factor analysis is the most common method, but other methods are also possible, such as cluster analysis of attributes. When applied to multiple variables assessed in a sample of individuals, these methods derive groupings of attributes that reflect the actual covariation among the scores for the attributes in that particular sample. If the sample is large enough to be statistically reliable and is representative of a particular population, the results constitute empirically derived prototypes, consisting of lists of features that tend to cooccur in that population. Because human attributes are seldom perfectly correlated with one another, few individuals manifest all the features of an empirically derived prototype. The number of features of an empirically derived prototype that an individual manifests, however, can provide an index of the degree to which he or she matches the prototype.

Empirically derived prototypes reflect the *actual covariation* among features in samples of individuals. Conceptual prototypes, by contrast, reflect the features that people *think of* as occurring together. Conceptual prototypes may accurately reflect covariation among features or they may not. There is no way of knowing, however, whether conceptual prototypes accurately reflect covariation among features without actually assessing covariation among the features occurring in a sample of cases. It is therefore desirable to base prototypes of disorders on empirical assessment of covariation among the features of actual cases. The study of borderline personality discussed earlier showed that the criterial features and cutoff point (five out of eight features) required for *DSM*-III diagnoses do not necessarily match the target phenomena (Clarkin et al., 1983). If this is true for an adult diagnostic category, it may be even more true for child diagnostic categories, which are complicated by developmental issues and the need for sources of data other than clinical interviews with the person being diagnosed.

Chapter 4 pointed out that some multivariate prototypes resemble the lists of descriptive features specified for *DSM* child and adolescent disorders (see Table 4.3). The similarity between the *DSM* categories and the empirically derived prototypes is limited, however, by the lack of empirical basis for the *DSM*'s descriptive features and cutoff points. Furthermore, the lack of *DSM* categories for some empirically derived syndromes and vice versa suggests gaps between the conceptual prototypes and the phenomena they are intended to capture.

Metrification of Prototypes

Research on conceptual prototypes demonstrates a quantitative basis for categorization, in that people's assignment of cases to a category depends on the number of the category's features that the cases manifest. In conceptual prototypes, however, the selection and enumeration of features is not based on empirical assessment of quantitative relations among features. Instead, the quantitative basis for categorization remains implicit, in that people categorize cases according to their impressions of the overlap with prototypes.

Judgments of the presence versus absence of each feature are also apt to be based on quantitative aspects of each feature, because a feature is most likely to be judged present when it is especially salient, intense, or otherwise evident in high degree. Although some features may truly exist in present-versus-absent form, even these are subject to quantitative variations in people's awareness of them. A problem behavior such as firesetting, for example, might be categorized as either present or absent. If a child sets and extinguishes a single minor fire while playing with matches, however, both the probability of detection and judgment of whether the problem behavior is present are less likely than if a child is observed to set ten serious fires. In categorizing a child's behavior problems, quantitative considerations are thus involved in our awareness of each criterial feature, which in turn affects the number of features judged present and, hence, the degree to which a case matches a category.

If quantification is implicit in our judgments of criterial attributes as well as in our categorization of cases, why not make it explicit? Although neither the features of syndromes nor the syndromes themselves may be quantifiable with perfect precision, even crude metrification can advance assessment, the taxonic integration of assessment data, and, ultimately, our ability to understand and ameliorate child and adolescent psychopathology.

As an illustration of the practical value of metrification, consider the use of speedometers to assess velocity. Many automobile speedometers are inaccurate by about 10%. The degree of inaccuracy varies from car to car and varies for a particular car as a function of speed, tire pressure, and tire size. Inaccuracies in reading speedometers also vary with their overall legibility, the angle from which drivers view them, and various characteristics of the driver—such as previous experience with the speedometer, fatigue, anxiety, impatience, and intoxication. Despite all the sources of error in judging speed from speedometers, the availability of a common metric makes it possible to integrate diverse sorts of information for a variety of related purposes.

Because all drivers can regulate their speed by reference to the same metric, speed limits can be set according to road conditions and experience with accident rates for particular speeds under those road conditions. The standard metric for speed is also used to design roads, including widths, grades, and curves, as well as cars, including engine and braking power, transmissions, and automatic speed control devices. The linking of so many variables through a common metric frees drivers to make more effective "clinical" judgments of unique conditions involving avoidance of accidents, decisions about the time needed to reach a particular destination, and the pleasure of high speed versus the costs in fuel, danger, and risk of arrest. Despite inaccuracies in judgments from speedometers, these judgments are far more effective than if people had to rely exclusively on their own subjective sense of speed. Similar benefits accrue from common devices for measuring weight, length, and temperature. Despite a lack of perfect precision in the devices and in the way people use them, they permit much more effective assessment and communication than if people had to judge and describe weight, length, and temperature in purely subjective terms, varying from person to person and situation to situation.

The reader may already have guessed where the argument is heading. It can be summarized up to this point as follows:

(1) Mental categories are based largely on conceptual prototypes, characterized by groups of features assumed to be mutually correlated.

(2) Categorization involves judgments of the degree to which the features of an individual case correspond to the prototypic features of a category.

(3) The judgment of correspondence between an individual case and a category is implicitly quantitative, based on the number and weighting of prototypic features judged to be present in the case.

(4) Judgments of each prototypic feature are also implicitly quantitative, in that salience, intensity, and rate of occurrence affect judgments of the feature's presence versus absence.

(5) Metrification can greatly improve the reliability of assessment and interpersonal communication, thereby freeing human minds to concentrate on "clinical" judgments of complex and unique situations that are not susceptible to metrification.

(6) Prototypes of child and adolescent disorders can be derived empirically through multivariate methods.

(7) The similarity between individual cases and empirically derived prototypes can be computed from scores based on (a) the *number* of prototypic

features detected in the case and (b) the *degree to which* each feature is evident.

If we accept the empirical derivation of prototypes by quantitative methods and the metrification of assessment for determining the similarity between individual cases and prototypes, it is worth considering possibilities for more extensive metrification of assessment and taxonomy, as discussed next.

TAXOMETRY

There is little doubt that humans have a natural inclination to think in terms of categories. Categorical thinking is one way of chunking information to cope with multiple variables and the different values that each variable can assume. Because categorical thinking is so pervasive, it is natural to think that the world is composed of neat, categorical units. Yet cognitive research shows that mental categorization involves a quantitative matching of individual cases to prototypes. Quantitative variations in criterial features are also apt to affect our judgments of which features are present or absent. These quantitative underpinnings of categorical judgments show that there is no intrinsic contradiction between categorical and quantitative approaches to assessment and taxonomy. Instead, they suggest that more explicit use of quantitative aids can greatly strengthen assessment and taxonomy, as well as the links between them. To appreciate the possibilities more fully, let us move beyond the metrification of prototypes and view the overall structure of taxonomy from a metrical perspective.

The term "taxometry" emphasizes quantitative aspects of attributes and cases, in contrast to viewing cases as all-or-none exemplars of mutually exclusive categories. The term "taxometrics" has previously been applied to the use of cluster analysis for classifying complex entities such as biological species (Sneath & Sokal, 1973) and to classification of people hypothesized to have a genotype for schizophrenia (schizotypes) via psychometric procedures for discriminating them from nonschizotypes (Meehl & Golden, 1982). In both instances, however, quantitative methods are viewed as aids to the categorization of cases in an ultimately yes or no fashion, corresponding to classical, nonquantitative taxonomies. The notion of taxometry proposed here does not deny that some disorders may exist in a categorical, present-versus-absent form, and that quantitative methods may help to determine which individuals have disorders of this sort. However, taxometric approaches can make broader contributions to our understanding of child and adolescent disorders, as well as to the methodology of assessment and taxonomy.

Taxometry of Disorders Assumed to Be Categorical

Even if a disorder truly exists in categorical form, incomplete knowledge of its specific etiology or a lack of definitive diagnostic techniques argue for metrification to maximize the utility of assessment and taxonomy. If categories are imposed without knowledge of the true boundaries of disorders, some individuals who have the disorders will be treated like those who do not. Conversely, some who really do not have the disorders will be treated like those who do. Metrical procedures for assessing and grouping disorders, on the other hand, can more sensitively reflect both the quantitative variations in phenotypic indicators of an underlying categorical disorder and the probabilistic nature of imperfect indicators of the disorder. Where multiple indicators are scored in degrees and their scores are aggregated into a total score, individuals with the highest scores are the most likely to have the disorder. Conversely, those with the lowest scores are least likely to have the disorder. This is true whether the aggregated indicators vary quantitatively or probabilistically with the underlying disorder.

According to prototype views of categories, the accuracy with which a case is recognized as a member of a category is a function of the degree to which it manifests prototypic features. Using a quantitative index of prototypic features, we can regard cases having the highest scores as the most likely true positives and those with the lowest scores as the most likely true negatives. Decisions about cases with intermediate scores can be based on the relative disadvantages of false positive and false negative misclassifications. If incorrectly classifying cases as positive has serious disadvantages, the cutoff point can be set high on the distribution of total scores for prototypic features, thereby minimizing the risk of false positives. If, on the other hand, incorrectly classifying cases as negative has serious disadvantages, the cutoff point can be set low to reduce the risk of false negatives.

A further benefit of quantifying prototypic features is that we can identify intermediate scores for which no classification decisions should be made without additional data. Even with additional data, some cases should perhaps not be classified as either positive or negative with respect to the disorder in question. Clearly marking such cases as intermediate or unclassifiable may be preferable to incorrectly classifying them as positive or negative. Diagnoses such as schizophrenia, for example, carry the stigma of incurability. Because premature diagnosis may unduly stigmatize a child without necessarily conferring any benefits, it is important to avoid jumping to diagnostic conclusions in ambiguous cases. Decisions about cutoff points for demarcating negative, unclassifiable, and positive cases should, of course, be validated against criteria external to the assessment procedures used to obtain the scores. Quantitative indices of a taxon, however, can be calibrated against external criteria much more efficiently than can purely categorical classifications, which fail to differentiate between borderline and extreme instances of a type.

As an illustration, Edelbrock (1984) used a structured parent interview (the DISC-P) to obtain DSM-III diagnostic data on clinically referred children. Cases were grouped according to whether they failed to meet the DSM criteria for a diagnosis, they met the minimum number of descriptive features required for the diagnosis, or they exceeded the minimum. To relate the three "levels" of each diagnosis to an external criterion, Edelbrock compared the mean scores obtained by the three groups on the empirically derived syndrome scales of the Child Behavior Profile (Achenbach & Edelbrock, 1983). Figure 6.1 shows the relation between cases grouped by three levels of DSM-III diagnoses and their scores on the empirically derived scales that are most similar to the DSM diagnoses. T scores above 70 represent the clinical range of the empirically derived Child Behavior Profile scales.

As Figure 6.1 shows, cases grouped according to three levels of DSM-III diagnoses (none, mild, severe) had progressively higher scores on the corresponding Child Behavior Profile scales. Furthermore, cases not meeting the DSM-III criteria had T scores averaging below 70, whereas those meeting or exceeding the criteria had T scores averaging 70 or higher.

Taxometry of Disorders Not Assumed to Be Categorical

Despite the categorical structure of DSM-III and the potential advantages of metrification even with a categorical system, there is little reason to assume that most child and adolescent disorders truly exist in a categorical form, such that all cases can be definitively divided into two classes: those who do and those who do not have a particular disorder. Instead, it is more likely that causal factors operate in varying combinations and degrees. It is also likely that their effects depend on

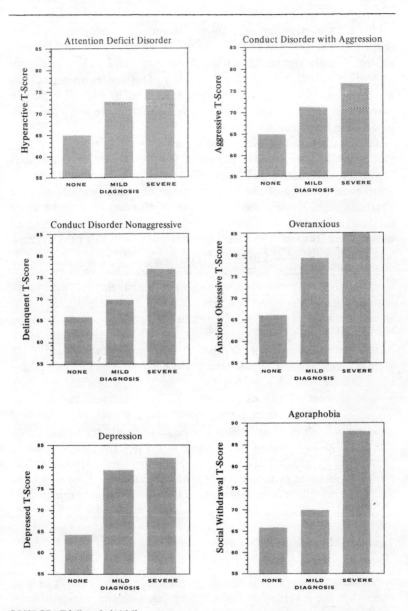

SOURCE: Edelbrock (1984).
NOTE: A T score of 70 is the upper limit of the normal range on scales of the Child Behavior Profile.

Figure 6.1   Relations Between DSM-III Syndrome Scores from the DISC-P and T Scores on Corresponding Scales of the Child Behavior Profile

multiple characteristics of children, including developmental level, constitutional strengths and vulnerabilities, competencies, and temperament. Family dynamics, supports, stresses, and role models are important as well. Considering the variety of influences on most childhood disorders and the quantitative variations in such disorders, a taxometric approach can be especially helpful where there are no a priori categorical commitments.

Rather than starting with a priori constructs and criteria, a taxometric approach starts with a large pool of features. Quantitative methods are used to determine which features are statistically associated with one another in samples of the target population, such as children of a particular age. As described in Chapter 4, this can be done by using methods such as factor analysis to identify syndrome-like groupings of cooccurring features. The resulting syndromes constitute prototypes to which individual cases can be matched.

By using the same instrument to assess individual children as was used to derive the syndromes, we can operationally define the degree to which each child manifests features of each prototypic syndrome—that is, we can employ standardized procedures to obtain a score expressing the child's standing on each syndrome. By obtaining distributions of scores in normative samples or other reference groups, we can determine a child's standing not only in terms of the absolute quantity of prototypic features but also relative to the scores of a standard reference group. A score of 10 out of a possible 16 prototypic features, for example, tells us little unless we know that the average for normal children is 2 out of 16 and that only 5% of clinically referred children score as high as 10 out of 16. Unlike a priori taxonomic constructs, a taxometric approach thus derives prototypic syndromes from quantitative data obtained with assessment procedures that can then be used to gauge the resemblance of new cases to the prototypic syndromes.

Taxometric Integration of Prototypic Syndromes

Viewing disorders as quantifiable prototypic syndromes can help us cope with the diversity of maladaptive behavior that children often display. Nonquantitative categorical systems, such as the *DSM*, handle this through multiple diagnoses of the same child, although the *DSM* excludes certain diagnoses when the criteria for other diagnoses are met. The exclusion rules are not empirically based, however, and Costello et al. (1984) found that they contained too many mutual contradictions to be applied as stated in *DSM*-III. Furthermore, the use of multiple diagnoses for children who have a variety of problem behavior implies that the children are suffering from several distinct disorders, whereas the different kinds of problem behavior may be closely interrelated. When different kinds of problem behavior are present, diagnosticians also tend to ignore those that are inconsistent with the category uppermost in their mind, as was found in the study of depression discussed earlier (Horowitz, Post et al., 1981).

To preserve data on multiple prototypic syndromes, the syndromes can be scored in a profile format. If we accept the metrification of syndromes, we can view a child in terms of the degree of deviance manifested on each relevant syndrome. The integration of empirically derived syndromes in a profile format was illustrated with the Child Behavior Profile shown in Figure 4.1. Normative data for the syndrome scales of this profile make it possible to portray a child's standing on each syndrome in terms of norm-based standard scores and percentiles. It is thus easy to compare the child's degree of deviance from one syndrome to another.

Although a fully taxometric approach starts with the quantitative derivation of syndromes, as done for the Child Behavior Profile, syndromes constructed in other ways can also be displayed in a profile format. Thus, for example, if normative data were obtained for the descriptive features of *DSM* syndromes, norm-based standard scores could be computed and displayed in a profile format. Because many disturbed children meet the criteria for multiple *DSM* diagnoses, and children meeting the criteria for a particular diagnosis vary in severity (see Figure 6.1), profiles can improve the integration of data even for *DSM* syndromes. Rather than risking the information-processing biases arising from forced choices between categories differing in salience, a profile of scores simultaneously compares the child's standing on multiple syndromes. This equalizes attention to each syndrome, as well as revealing patterns characterized by deviance in several areas. Such patterns may convey a much better picture of a child's overall problems than do multiple categorical diagnoses.

The use of profiles to display multiple dimensions is, of course, not new. The assessment of diagnostic constructs in terms of multidimensional profiles is not new either, as the MMPI has long done this. The MMPI, however, is based on Kraepelinian diagnostic constructs and is designed to aid in categorical diagnostic judgments by discriminating between those who do and those who do not have scores above certain cutoffs on particular scales. Where we lack well-established diagnostic categories, however, multidimensional profiles can contribute to the derivation of the constructs themselves. That is, if we construct syndromes taxometrically, the syndromes consist of prototypic features actually found to covary. Profiles can then integrate scores on multiple syndromes to reflect the overall patterns displayed by individuals. These patterns can provide the basis for typologies of individuals.

Taxometric Typologies

Profiles of syndrome scores can avoid the information-processing biases arising when we infer categorical disorders from features that do not actually occur in all-or-none categorical form. Certain profile patterns, such as exceptional elevations on the Psychopathic Deviate and Manic scales of the MMPI, may suggest categorical diagnoses, such as antisocial personality. Yet the advantages of profiles for displaying patterns and degrees of disorders may be lost if we cannot take account of the quantitative variations thus preserved, or if we impose categories that miss important differences between profile patterns. Granting the need to simplify complex data, how can we retain important distinctions that are lost when we categorize?

Many current technological advances depend on innovative ways of simplifying large masses of data. In medical diagnosis, for example, computed tomography (CT scanning) integrates masses of complex assessment data into much more informative images of inner structures than are feasible with noncomputerized techniques. The basic principle of computerized integration of multivariate data has many specialized applications. In single photon emission computed tomography (SPECT), for example, a camera designed to detect radioactivity from drugs in the body rotates around the patient to make a series of images. The images are then integrated and displayed in three-dimensional form by a computer.

Computers are also used to integrate large quantities of multivariate data from EEGs and evoked electrical responses in the brain to detect abnormalities of brain function that are revealed in wave patterns. An example at the interface of organic and behavioral pathology is the finding that boys at high risk for alcoholism (they have alcoholic fathers) differ from control boys in evoked electrical brain responses (Begleiter, Porjesz, Bihari, & Kissin, 1984). These differences were detected by factor analyzing data from brain recordings and then comparing the factor scores of the high-risk and control boys.

It may seem presumptuous to draw analogies between advanced biomedical technology and the taxometry of psychopathology. Despite the rudimentary stage of our knowledge, however, we face assessment tasks like those that have benefited greatly from information-processing technology. These tasks involve the use of multiple low-grade data points to extract a meaningful "signal" from a background of random "noise." Our data may include ratings by parents and teachers, self-reports by children during interviews, observations of children, responses to psychological and educational tests, and medical data.

Medical data may be decisive for pinpointing organic abnormalities, but such data are seldom decisive in the assessment of children and adolescents referred for mental health services. Instead, it is necessary to construct an understanding of each case out of diverse kinds of nonmedical data. In effect, we develop a hypothetical construct of the individual case—a conceptual representation of the child's strengths and deficits, developmental history, family situation, possible causal factors, prognosis, and likely responsiveness to various therapies. To apply knowledge gained through research, training, and clinical experience, we need to link the individual case with similar cases. There are numerous possible criteria for linkage, but the child's sex, age and cognitive level should always be taken into account when seeking comparable cases. Within groups of a particular sex, age, and cognitive level (e.g., normal range versus educable retarded), typologies can be constructed by grouping children whose profiles show similar patterns of syndrome scores.

Chapter 4 discussed the use of cluster analysis to construct profile typologies (Figures 4.2 and 4.3 illustrate the results). The use of multivariate statistics, such as cluster analysis, to construct typologies of profile patterns is analogous to the derivation of syndromes through multivariate analysis of specific problems scored in a sample of individuals. Rather than being aimed at covariation of problems, however, taxometric typologies group individuals on the basis of similarities they manifest on multiple variables.

In the Chapter 4 illustration, each child had norm-based standard scores on nine syndromes that were previously derived through factor analysis of problems rated by parents of clinically referred children. Typologies can also be taxometrically derived from scores on other variables, such as ratings by teachers, observers, clinicians, or children themselves, cognitive and achievement tests, and measures of perceptual-motor and neurological functioning. Furthermore, the same children might be simultaneously classified by several typologies, each dealing with a particular assessment method.

Because behavior problems are often situationally specific, it may be desirable to have taxometric typologies derived separately from reports by different types of informants, such as parents and teachers. It would, of course, also be important to identify patterns that are associated with one another across situations. This can be done by combining profiles of scores from the different types of informants in a single cluster analysis. If a pattern found in data from one type of informant is consistently associated with a particular pattern found in data from the other type of informant, the two patterns would be joined in a single overarching type. However, there may be good reasons for keeping different domains separate in the assessment of individual children, as discussed later.

Taxometric Assignment of Individuals to Types

Using the cluster analytic approach described in Chapter 4, a child can be classified according to cluster-based types by computing intra-class correlations (ICCs) between the child's profile of syndrome scores and the *centroid* of each profile type. (The centroid is the profile formed by averaging the profiles of all members of a cluster. It constitutes the operational definition of the cluster-based profile type.) The ICC provides an objective, quantitative index of the degree to which a particular child's profile resembles a type, taking account of the entire pattern and elevation of the profile.

Because the ICC is objective, it is not vulnerable to information-processing biases arising in the mental assignment of cases to categories. Furthermore, because the ICC is quantitative, it enables us to view categorization in terms of degrees, rather than as a yes-or-no proposition. This applies the prototype concept of categories to profile patterns encompassing multiple syndromes that themselves are taxometrically derived prototypes.

The use of a quantitative index such as the ICC makes the quantitative prototypic nature of categorization explicit. It also highlights the fact that many individuals have features of more than one type, and it provides an objective basis for either choosing among categories or deciding against categorization of a particular case. That is, the user can consider a child's ICC with each relevant type and can choose the size of the ICC required for categorization. The user's clinical judgment, of course, remains crucial in deciding what will be done with taxometric findings.

A user can also require that the child have an ICC above the chosen cutoff with only one profile type. We can decide, for example, to view a child as having a particular profile type if the ICC exceeds .40 with one type and not any other type. The choice of the cutoff and exclusion of correlations with other types would depend on the user's aims. For many purposes, it is not worth precluding correlations with other profile types, because certain profile types are similar enough to merge when cluster analyses are carried out in a hierarchical fashion, as illustrated in Figure 4.3. If a child has a high ICC with two types, the two types are thus likely to be closely related. (For procedural details and the implications of various cutoff criteria, see Achenbach & Edelbrock, 1983; Edelbrock & Achenbach, 1980.)

Summary of Taxometry

The case for taxometry can be summarized as follows:

(1) Many important features vary quantitatively.
(2) Syndromes consist of features that are imperfectly correlated with one another, rather than occurring in an all-or-none fashion.
(3) Humans categorize cases according to quantitative impressions of prototypic features.
(4) Multivariate analyses can yield operational definitions of prototypic syndromes.
(5) Scores for the number and intensity of prototypic features operationally define a child's resemblance to a syndrome.
(6) Norm-based syndrome scores compare the child with peers.
(7) To integrate data on multiple prototypic syndromes, the syndromes can be embodied in a multidimensional profile.
(8) Taxometric typologies can be constructed by identifying groups of children having similar profile patterns.
(9) Individual children can be categorized on the basis of similiarity between their profiles and each of the profile types.
(10) Quantitative indices of similarity avoid information-processing biases that affect mental categorization; they permit categorization to reflect degrees of prototypicality.
(11) Taxometry capitalizes on computerized data processing to obtain norm-based standard scores for syndromes, profile types, and quantitative indices of similarity to profile types.
(12) The taxometric aggregation of standardized assessment data enables the clinician to concentrate more on the many aspects of assessment and treatment that cannot be standardized.

MULTIAXIAL FACETS OF TAXONIC INTEGRATION

Taxometry derives taxonomic distinctions directly from particular assessment procedures. The data are obtained, scored, and analyzed in a standardized fashion for all cases. This differs from most taxonomies of psychopathology, which leave the diagnostician to decide what data to obtain and how to use them to categorize disorders. An exception is the diagnosis of mental retardation, which requires an IQ below a certain level (usually 70) on an individually administered IQ test. The *DSM*-III even designated four "subtypes" of retardation according to IQ: *Mild retardation*—IQ 50-70; *Moderate*—IQ 35-49; *Severe*—IQ 20-34; *Profound*—IQ below 20 (APA, 1980).

The use of standardized IQ tests to diagnose mental retardation can be viewed as a limited application of taxometry. Despite the centrality of IQ in the diagnosis of retardation, however, other types of data are also used to judge whether a low IQ accurately represents a child's adaptive capabilities, whether there is an identifiable organic cause for the retardation, and whether the child has other diagnosable conditions. The other data typically include a developmental history, interview or other clinical observations of the child, medical assessments, and reports from significant adults, such as parents and teachers. The clinician must ultimately integrate all these data in a comprehensive case formulation.

A similar range of variables must be considered in other disorders as well. Multiaxial systems have been devised to focus attention on different kinds of relevant variables. As discussed in Chapter 4, the taxonomy of childhood disorders proposed by a World Health Organization seminar provides four axes (Rutter et al., 1975), whereas the *DSM* and *ICD*-9 provide five axes. It is thus recognized that no one set of taxonomic concepts—such as psychiatric syndromes—provides an adequate diagnostic picture.

Proposed Axes for Child and Adolescent Disorders

Whatever assessment and taxonomic approaches we favor, multiple axes can help in separating the different facets of functioning relevant to psychopathology. For children, different facets involve different life arenas, different sources of data, and different modes of assessment. Table 6.1 summarizes axes based on five facets of assessment and taxonomy. These axes are not intended as a final system for achieving all

TABLE 6.1
Examples of Multiaxial Assessment and Taxonomy

Age Range	Axis I Parent Perceptions	Axis II Teacher Perceptions	Axis III Cognitive Assessment	Axis IV Physical Conditions	Axis V Clinician's Assessment
0-2	developmental history Minnesota Child Development Inventory* (Ireton & Thwing, 1974)	—	Bayley (1969) Infant Scales	height, weight, neurological and medical exam	observations during developmental testing
2-5	developmental history Child Behavior Checklist* (Achenbach & Edelbrock, 1983) Louisville Behavior Checklist* (Miller, 1981)	Kohn (1977) Symptom Checklist* Preschool Behavior Checklist* (Behar & Stringfield, 1974)	McCarthy (1972) Scales*	height, weight, neurological and medical exam	observations during play interview
6-11	developmental history Child Behavior Checklist* Louisville Behavior Checklist*	CBCL-Teacher's Report Form* (Edelbrock & Achenbach, 1984) School Behavior Checklist* (Miller, 1972)	achievement tests* Kaufman (1983) Assessment Battery* Koppitz (1975) Bender Gestalt WISC-R* (Wechsler, 1981)	height, weight, neurological and medical exam	Child Assessment Schedule (Hodges et al., 1982) * Semistructured Clinical Interview for Children* (Achenbach & McConaughy, 1985)
12-18	developmental history Child Behavior Checklist* Louisville Behavior Checklist*	CBCL-Teacher's Report Form* School Behavior Checklist*	achievement tests* WISC-R* WAIS-R* (Wechsler, 1981)	height, weight, neurological and medical exam	DISC* (Costello et al., 1984) Youth Self-Report* (Achenbach & Edelbrock, 1983)

NOTE: Where multiple instruments are available, those with the most promising reliability, validity, and normative data are listed.
*Taxometric approach feasible.

173

goals of assessment and taxonomy. Instead, they offer a model for organizing aspects of assessment and taxonomy that are particularly relevant to children. In keeping with the differential roles of different kinds of data, each axis primarily concerns a particular kind of data. Findings represented by each axis are not necessarily expected to converge on any single taxonomic construct, but to present in mosaic fashion a child's functioning in different areas as assessed by methods appropriate to those areas. Each axis can encompass taxonomic constructs specific to its own type of assessment.

Axis I: Parent Perceptions

A key arena for all children is the family, for which parents and parent surrogates are the main sources of data. Because it is seldom feasible to directly assess home behavior in a comprehensive and nonreactive way, and because parents' perceptions constitute a key aspect of the problems to be treated, parents' reports form one taxonomic axis. The taxometric research discussed earlier demonstrates how standardized reports from parents can be used to derive syndromes and typologies of disorders and competencies.

Axis II: Teacher Perceptions

Once children reach school age, the school becomes a second key arena, for which teachers become the primary informants. Like parent reports, standardized reports by teachers yield assessment data from which to derive syndromes and typologies of school behavior, as perceived by the teachers. Because direct and nonreactive observational assessment is often more feasible in schools than in homes, observational procedures can be used to supplement teacher reports, although teacher reports provide a more uniform basis for norm-based typologies (Edelbrock & Achenbach, 1985).

Axis III: Cognitive Measures

The third axis concerns the child's cognitive functioning, as assessed by standardized tests. Intellectual level is a separate axis in the WHO and *ICD*-9 systems. *DSM*-III included mental retardation with psychiatric syndromes as an Axis I category, with subtypes defined in terms of IQ scores. As argued by Rutter and Shaffer (1980), however, it makes more sense to view intellectual level as a continuous dimension on which all scores are important, rather than viewing it only in terms of arbitrary cutoff points for defining retardation as a disorder. An IQ of 150 is thus considered in our overall judgment of a child, just as much as the IQ scores that are used to demarcate retardation. Furthermore, rather than being considered a disorder comparable to psychiatric syndromes, low ability is an important facet of the child's functioning in its own right, which may or may not be accompanied by identifiable disorders.

Although IQ provides a simple operational definition of ability, the concept of a diagnostic axis is broad enough to encompass other aspects of cognitive functioning. This axis can thus be used to list not only the child's IQ, but also other important measures of cognitive functioning, such as achievement and perceptual-motor tests, which can be summarized thusly: IQ = 120; Composite Achievement Score = 70th percentile; Koppitz (1975) Perceptual-Motor Score = 9 years.

Axis IV: Physical Conditions

Another axis is represented in the *DSM* as physical disorders or conditions, in the WHO taxonomy as biological factors, and in *ICD*-9 as somatic symptomatology. These are clearly important to note when assessing psychopathology, but the taxonomic issues here are similar to those of general medical taxonomy. Beside physical abnormalities, however, age-based percentiles for parameters such as height and weight, as well as neurological "soft signs," are useful to list here. This highlights physical deviations that should be considered in the overall case formulation.

Axis V: Clinician's Assessment

The final axis concerns the clinician's own personal assessment of the child and family, as they express themselves to the clinician. Granting the need for clinicians to form first-hand impressions of each case, how can we improve the reliability, validity, and utility of direct clinical assessment? The clinical interview with the child is the most universal assessment procedure and the one that we would be most loathe to omit before drawing diagnostic conclusions. Yet it is one of the least validated procedures, and its reliability is limited by variations in clinicians' effects on children, their interview techniques, and the way in which they draw conclusions from interviews.

Efforts to improve the yield of child interviews have tended toward two extremes. At one extreme, highly structured questions are asked about the specific symptoms, as exemplified by the DISC (Costello et al, 1984). At the other extreme, unstructured interviews are used as a basis for making more global judgments about the child, as exemplified by the Mental Health Assessment Form (Kestenbaum & Bird, 1978).

Below a mental age of about 11, it is hard for children to interpret structured questions about their problems, consider all the relevant aspects of their experience, and formulate accurate answers. Such difficulties are reflected in a test-retest correlation of .43 for 6-9-year-olds' responses to the DISC (Edelbrock, Costello, Dulcan, Kalas, & Conover, 1985). The reliability of children's responses increases with age, as indicated by a test-retest correlation of .60 for 10-13-year-olds and .71 for 14-18-year-olds. Young children show a particularly marked tendency to change their responses from affirmative during an initial interview to negative during a repeat interview several days later. Edelbrock et al. (1985) found, for example, that DISC symptom scores declined 33% in test-retest interviews with 6-9-year-old children, 24% with 10-13-year-olds, and 16% with 14-18-year-olds.

Adolescents' greater ability to grasp structured interview questions does not necessarily mean that it is easy to gain their confidence and candor. However, self-report checklists analogous to those used to obtain taxometric data from parents and teachers can be used to obtain data similar to structured interviews, while avoiding the interpersonal obstacles arising in face-to-face interviews with adolescents (Achenbach & Edelbrock, 1983). With younger children, we face not only the problem of rapport, but that of adapting clinical assessment to their cognitive levels. This means that both the format and goals of clinical assessment must be geared to children's abilities.

With infants and toddlers, developmental tests such as the Bayley and Gesell scales represent the most feasible form of direct clinical assessment. These measures provide opportunities for judging the child's overall emotional tone and developmental progress in domains such as motor functioning, language, perception, simple problem solving, and social relatedness. Similar formats and goals apply to preschoolers, although play sessions accompanied by some questioning can broaden clinical assessment as preschoolers advance socially and cognitively.

From the limited range of direct clinical assessment feasible in the early years, the elementary school period expands the possibilities considerably, as children's social and communication skills advance. However, the unreliability of elementary school children's responses to highly structured questions and the inconsistent yield of unstructured interviews argue for hybrid approaches to direct clinical assessment during the elementary school period. This requires considerable flexibility with individual children and allowance for case-to-case variation. One approach is a semistructured interview format, using prescribed open-ended questions to cover particular domains, such as school, home, peer relations, feelings about the self, anxieties, aspirations, and fantasies. Asking children to draw pictures of their family can also encourage expression of feelings and perceptions that are difficult to reach through direct questions. School-related tasks, such as individual achievement tests, can be included to sample children's ways of coping with academic demands.

Taxometry of Interview Data

Even though the precise course of semistructured interviews and the specific wording of questions may vary from case to case, it is possible to apply standardized taxometric procedures to the scoring and aggregation of the data. This is exemplified in research by Achenbach and McConaughy (1985), who developed separate instruments for rating what 6- to 11-year-old children say and do during semistructured clinical interviews. The ratings form the basis for taxometric procedures like those described earlier for parent and teacher ratings. From this research, it is evident that what some children do is much more informative than what they say, whereas other children show the reverse pattern. There is a developmental trend in these patterns, with verbal self-reports growing more dominant after the age of about 8. However, some younger children convey more by words than by action; conversely, some older children convey more by action than by words. Direct clinical assessment must therefore be broad enough to encompass the wide variations found in elementary school age children. The taxometric use of interviews thus requires recognition that their yield varies from case to case and must be integrated with other assessment procedures.

Because clinical impressions from interviews are so salient, it is especially necessary to guard against the information-processing biases to which they are vulnerable. Taxometric techniques can help to do this. The profile patterns derived from adolescents' checklist responses and elementary school children's interviews may be especially helpful in selecting treatments. For example, the degree to which a child verbalizes problems or acts out problems may indicate the degree to which talking therapies versus other approaches are feasible. It must be kept in mind, however, that the power of taxometric typologies to standardize, quantify, and integrate large quantities of assessment data does not eliminate the clinician's role in deriving comprehensive case formulations. On the contrary, taxometric approaches should help clinicians make more accurate case formulations by reducing information overload, subjective biases, and inappropriate categorization.

IMPLICATIONS FOR CLINICAL SERVICES AND RESEARCH

The foregoing material may seem abstract, but it has the following implications for clinical services and research:

(1) The multiple facets of children's functioning require multiple assessment procedures, which need not converge on a single categorical construct for each child. Instead, each of the axes outlined in Table 6.1 can fulfill a taxonomic function with respect to particular types of assessment. Other axes may also be feasible, such as a separate one for family functioning.

(2) Certain axes will occasionally be irrelevant or uninformative, such as Axis II (teacher perceptions) if the child is not attending school and Axis IV (physical conditions) if there are no organic abnormalities. Nevertheless, the multiaxial perspective highlights each facet in its own right, rather than collapsing them all into a single categorical construct. Differences in the way children are seen by their parents, teachers, and clinicians can thus be highlighted rather than obscured.

(3) Within Axes I, II, and V (parent, teacher, and clinician assessments), taxometric methods can objectively classify children according to profile types that are scored from standardized assessment procedures. IQ, achievement, and perceptual-motor tests provide an analogous basis for Axis III classification.

(4) By using the same standardized assessment procedures for clinical and research taxometry, the clinical utility of research findings can be greatly enhanced.

(5) The same standardized taxometric procedures can be used in epidemiological studies of the distribution of specific problems, syndromes, and profile patterns, thereby linking epidemiology directly to clinical practice and research.

(6) Taxometric assessments can be repeated to measure developmental changes and the effects of interventions.

(7) The definition of disorders for purposes of third-party payment is an increasingly critical problem that can only be remedied by improving the empirical basis for defining and treating disorders.

(8) If the rationale for the taxometric approach is accepted, the following research warrants high priority:

(a) Completion of taxometric procedures for clinicians' assessments of children and adolescents.

(b) Testing of relations between taxometric classifications made on different axes to determine whether multiaxial patterns are worth using (e.g., apply cluster analysis to profiles that include dimensions scored from parent, teacher, and clinician instruments).

(c) Testing of correlates of profile types, including possible etiological factors, typical course and outcome, and responsiveness to different treatments.

SUMMARY

Taxonomies are classifications intended to reflect intrinsic similarities and differences between cases. Cognitive research shows that taxonomic judgments involve quantitatively matching the features of individual cases to the prototypic features of categories. Clinicians' diagnostic judgments conform more closely to prototype models of categories than to categorization based on necessary and sufficient features. In effect, there is a quantitative basis for diagnostic judgment, whereby the number of prototypic features manifested by a case largely determines the diagnosis. In cases with few prototypic features, diagnostic reliability is reduced when some diagnosticians infer a categorical disorder in an all-or-none fashion, whereas others do not.

Prototypes can be empirically derived through multivariate analyses of covariation among features scored in samples of cases. The quantification implicit in diagnostic judgments can be made explicit by scoring the number and intensity of prototypic features manifested by each case.

Taxometry refers to the metrification of the taxonomic process, as exemplified by the following sequence: (1) quantitative scoring of descriptive features; (2) derivation of prototypical syndromes through multivariate analyses of these scores; (3) transformation of raw syndrome scores into norm-based standard scores; (4) aggregation of syndrome scores in multidimensional profiles; (5) construction of typologies of profile patterns through cluster analysis; and (6) classification of children according to quantitative indices of their resemblance to profile types. Like computerized biomedical assessment, computerized taxometry integrates multiple data points to highlight a common "signal" against a background of random "noise." This frees the clinician to concentrate on aspects of assessment and treatment that cannot be standardized.

The need to consider multiple facets of children's functioning argues for multiaxial approaches to assessment and taxonomy. Five axes were outlined for representing children's functioning in terms of different foci of assessment: Axis I—parent perceptions; Axis II—teacher perceptions; Axis III—cognitive measures; Axis IV—physical conditions; Axis V—clinician's assessment. Axes I, II, and V lend themselves to taxometry of behavioral problems and competencies in most age groups, whereas standardized ability and achievement tests exemplify taxometric approaches to Axis III assessment. Multiaxial taxometric approaches can help clinicians make accurate case formulations by reducing information overload, subjective biases, and inappropriate categorization.

A multiaxial taxometric approach has the following implications for clinical services and research:

(1) The multiple facets of children's functioning require multiple assessment procedures, which need not converge on a single categorical construct for each child.
(2) Although not all axes will be informative in every case, different facets of functioning are highlighted, instead of being collapsed into a single categorical construct.
(3) Taxometric methods can objectively classify children according to profile types scored from standardized assessment procedures for most axes.
(4) Use of a common set of standardized procedures can draw clinical practice and research closer together.
(5) Use of these same standardized procedures for epidemiological studies can link epidemiology more directly to clinical practice and research.
(6) Taxometric assessments can be repeated to measure developmental changes and the effects of interventions.
(7) Taxometric approaches can improve the basis for third-party reimbursement.
(8) Acceptance of the taxometric approach argues for the following kinds of research: completion of taxometric procedures for clinicians' assessments; testing of relations between taxometric classification on different axes; and testing of correlates of profile types.

REFERENCES

Achenbach, T. M. (1966). The classification of children's psychiatric symptoms: A factor-analytic study. *Pscyhological Monographs, 80* (615).

Achenbach, T. M. (1978). The Child Behavior Profile: I. Boys aged 6-11. *Journal of Consulting and Clinical Psychology, 46,* 478-488.

Achenbach, T. M. (1982). *Developmental psychopathology* (2nd ed.). New York: John Wiley.

Achenbach, T. M., Conners, C. K., & Quay, H. C. (1985). The ACQ Behavior Checklist. Burlington: University of Vermont. (Unpublished)

Achenbach, T. M., & Edelbrock, C. S. (1978). The classification of child psychopathology: A review and analysis of empirical efforts. *Psychological Bulletin, 85,* 1275-1301.

Achenbach, T. M., & Edelbrock, C. S. (1979). The Child Behavior Profile: II. Boys aged 12-16 and girls aged 6-11 and 12-16. *Journal of Consulting and Clinical Psychology, 47,* 223-233.

Achenbach, T. M., & Edelbrock, C. S. (1981). Behavioral problems and competencies reported by parents of normal and disturbed children aged four through sixteen. *Monographs of the Society for Research in Child Development, 46* (188).

Achenbach, T. M., & Edelbrock, C. S. (1983). *Manual for the Child Behavior Checklist and Revised Child Behavior Profile.* Burlington: University of Vermont.

Achenbach, T. M., & McConaughy, S. H. (1985). *Child Interview Checklist-Self Report Form; Child Interview Checklist-Observation Form.* Burlington: University of Vermont.

Achenbach, T. M., & Weisz, J. R. (1975) Impulsivity-reflectivity and cognitive development in preschoolers: A longitudinal analysis of developmental and trait variance. *Develomental Psychology, 11,* 413-414.

Ackerman, N. W. (1968). The role of the family in the emergence of child disorders. In E. Miller (Ed.), *Foundations of child psychiatry.* New York: Pergamon.

Ackerman, N. W., & Behrens, M. L. (1974). Family diagnosis and clinical process. In S. Arieti (Ed.), *Handbook of American psychiatry* (Vol. 2). New York: Basic Books.

Ackerson, L. (1931). *Children's behavior problems* (Vol. 1). Chicago: University of Chicago Press.

Ackerson, L. (1942). *Children's behavior problems* (Vol. 2). Chicago: University of Chicago Press.

Adelman, H. S., & Taylor, L. (1983). Classifying students by inferred motivation to learn. *Learning Disability Quarterly, 6,* 201-206.

American Academy of Child Psychiatry (1983). *Child psychiatry: A plan for the coming decades.* Washington, DC: Author.

American Association on Mental Deficiency (1981). *Adaptive Behavior Scales.* Monterey, CA: CTB/McGraw-Hill.

American Psychiatric Association (1952). *Diagnostic and statistical manual of mental disorders* (1st ed.). Washington, DC: Author.

American Psychiatric Association (1968). *Diagnostic and statistical manual of mental disorders* (2nd ed.) Washington, DC: Author.

American Psychiatric Association (1980). *Diagnostic and statistical manual of mental disorders* (3rd ed.). Washington, DC: Author.

Arkes, H. R. (1981). Impediments to accurate clinical judgment and possible ways to minimize their impact. *Journal of Consulting and Clinical Psychology, 49,* 323-330.

Arkes, H. R., & Harkness, A. R. (1983). Estimates of contingency between two dichotomous variables. *Journal of Experimental Psychology: General, 112,* 117-135.

Arkes, H. R., Harkness, A. R., & Biber, D. (1980). Salience and the judgment of contingency. Paper presented at the Midwestern Psychological Association, St. Louis.

Auerbach, A. H., & Luborsky, L. (1968). Accuracy of judgments and the nature of the "good hour." In J. M. Shlien (Eds.), *Research in psychotherapy: Vol. III.* Washington, DC: American Psychological Association.

Bayley, N. (1969). *Bayley Scales of Infant Development.* New York: Psychological Corporation.

Begleiter, H., Porjesz, B., Bihari, B., & Kissin, B. (1984). Event-related brain potentials in boys at risk for alcoholism. *Science, 225,* 1493-1496.

Behar, L. B., & Stringfield, S. (1974). A behavior rating scale for the preschool child. *Developmental Psychology, 10,* 601-610.

Beitchman, J. H., Dielman, T. E., Landis, J. R., Benson, R. M., & Kemp, P. L. (1978). Reliability of the Group for the Advancement of Psychiatry diagnostic categories in child psychiatry. *Archives of General Psychiatry, 35,* 1461-1466.

Bellack, A. S. (1979). A critical appraisal of strategies for assessing social skill. *Behavioral Assessment, 1,* 157-176.

Bellack, L., & Bellak, S. S. (1974). *Children's Apperception Test. Sixth and revised edition.* New York: CPS, Inc.

Binet, A., & Simon, T. (1916). New methods for the diagnosis of the intellectual level of subnormals. In A. Binet & T. Simon (Trans.), *The development of intelligence in children.* Baltimore: Williams & Wilkins. (Original work published 1905)

Bleuler, E. (1911). *Dementia praecox or the group of schizophrenias.* New York: International Universities Press.

Blouin, A.G.A., Bornstein, R. A., Trites, R. L. (1978). Alcohol use among hyperactive children: A five year follow-up study. *Journal of Pediatric Psychology, 3,* 188-194.

Blum, G. S. (1960). The Blacky Pictures with children. In A. I. Robin & M. R. Haworth (Eds.), *Projective techniques with children.* New York: Grune & Stratton.

Boll, T. J., & Barth, J. T. (1981). Neuropsychology of brain damage in children. In S. B. Filskov & T. J. Boll (Eds.), *Handbook of clinical neuropsychology.* New York: John Wiley.

Bolton, T. L. (1891). The growth of memory in school children. *American Journal of Psychology, 4,* 362-380.

Bower, E. M. (1969). *Early identification of emotionally handicapped children in school* (2nd ed.). Springfield, IL: Charles C Thomas.

Bradley, C. (1937). The behavior of children receiving benzedrine. *American Journal of Psychiatry, 94,* 577-585.

Brown, G. W., & Rutter, M. (1966). The measurement of family activities and relationships: A methodological study. *Human Relations, 19,* 241-263.

Brown, G., Chadwick, O., Shaffer, D., Rutter, M., & Traub, M. (1981). A prospective study of children with head injuries: III. Psychiatric sequelae. *Psychological Medicine, 11,* 63-78.

Buchsbaum, M., & Wender, P. (1973). Averaged evoked responses in normal and minimally brain dysfunctioned children treated with amphetamine. A preliminary report. *Archives of General Psychiatry, 29,* 764-770.

Burke, P. M., McCauley, E., Mitchell, J., & Smith, E. (1983). Dexamethasone suppression tests in children and adolescents. Presented at the American Academy of Child Psychiatry, San Francisco.

Cairns, E., & Cammock, T. (1978). Development of a more reliable version of the Matching Familiar Figures Test. *Developmental Psychology, 14,* 555-560.

Caldwell, B. M., & Bradley, R. H. (1979). *Home observation for measurement of the environment.* Little Rock: University of Arkansas at Little Rock, Center for Child Development and Education.

Cantor, N., Smith, E. E., French, R. deS., & Mezzich, J. (1980). Psychiatric diagnosis as prototype categorization. *Journal of Abnormal Psychology, 89,* 181-193.

Carlson, G. A., & Cantwell, D. P. (1982). Diagnosis of childhood depression: A comparison of the Weinberg and *DSM*-III criteria. *Journal of the American Academy of Child Psychiatry, 21,* 247-250.

Chandler, M. J., Paget, K. F., & Koch, D. A. (1978). The child's demystification of psychological defense mechanisms: A structural and developmental analysis. *Developmental Psychology, 14,* 197-205.

Chapman, L. J., & Chapman, J. P. (1967). Genesis of popular but erroneous psychodiagnostic observations. *Journal of Abnormal Psychology, 74,* 271-280.

Chapman, L. J., & Chapman, J. P. (1971). Associatively based illusory correlation as a source of psychodiagnostic folklore. In L. D. Goodstein & R. I. Lanyon (Eds.), *Readings in personality assessment.* New York: John Wiley.

Clarkin, J. F., Widiger, T. A., Frances, A., Hurt, S. W., & Gilmore, M. (1983). Prototypic typology and the borderline personality disorder. *Journal of Abnormal Psychology, 92,* 263-275.

Cohen, J. (1960). A coefficient of agreement for nominal scales. *Educational and Psychological Measurement, 20,* 37-46.

Cohen, J. (1968). Weighted kappa: Nominal scale agreement with provision for scaled disagreement or partial credit. *Psychological Bulletin, 70,* 213-220.

Coie, J. D., & Kupersmidt, J. B. (1983). A behavioral analysis of emerging social status in boys' groups. *Child Development, 54,* 1400-1416.

Conners, C. K. (1969). A teacher rating scale for use in drug studies with children. *American Journal of Psychiatry, 126,* 884-888.

Costello, A. J., Edelbrock, C., Dulcan, M. K., Kalas, R., & Kloric, S. H. (1984). Report on the diagnostic interview schedule for children (DISC). Pittsburgh: University of Pittsburgh.

Cytryn, L., & McKnew, D. H. (1979). Affective disorders. In J. Noshpitz (Ed.), *Basic handbook of child psychology* (Vol. 2). New York: Basic Books.

Cytryn, L., McKnew, D. H., & Bunney, W. E. (1980). Diagnosis of depression in children: A reassessment. *American Journal of Psychiatry, 137,* 22-25.

Dahlstrom, W. G., Welsh, G. S., & Dahlstrom, L. E. (1972). *An MMPI handbook, Vol. I: Clinical interpretation* (rev. ed.). Minneapolis: University of Minnesota Press.

Delong, G. R. (1978). Lithium carbonate treatment of select behavior disorders in children suggesting manic-depressive illness. *Journal of Pediatrics, 93,* 689-694.

Dmitruk, V. M., Collins, R. W., & Clinger, D. L. (1973). The "Barnum effect" and acceptance of negative personal evaluation. *Journal of Consulting and Clinical Psychology, 41,* 191-194.

Dodge, K. A. (1983). Behavioral antecedents of peer social status. *Child Development, 54,* 1386-1399.

Dodge, K. A. (in press). A social information processing model of social competence in children. In *Minnesota Symposium on Child Psychology.* Hillsdale, NJ: Erlbaum.

Doll, E. A. (1965). *Vineland social maturity scale.* Circle Pines, MN: American Guidance Service.

Dreger, R. M. (1981). First-, second-, and third-order factors from the children's behavioral classification instrument and an attempt at rapprochement. *Journal of Abnormal Psychology, 90,* 242-260.

Edelbrock, C. (1979). Mixture model tests of hierarchical clustering algorithms: The problem of classifying everybody. *Multivariate Behavioral Research, 14,* 367-384.

Edelbrock, C. (1984, October). Relations between the NIMH Diagnostic Interview Schedule for Children (DISC) and the Child Behavior Checklist and Profile. Presented at the American Academy of Child Psychiatry, Toronto.

Edelbrock, C., & Achenbach, T. M. (1980). A typology of Child Behavior Profile patterns: Distribution and correlates for disturbed children aged 6-16. *Journal of Abnormal Child Psychology, 8,* 441-470.

Edelbrock, C., & Achenbach, T. M. (1984). The teacher version of the Child Behavior Profile: I. Boys aged 6-11. *Journal of Consulting and Clinical Psychology, 52,* 207-217.

Edelbrock, C., & Achenbach, T. M. (1985). *Manual for the Teacher's Report Form and Teacher Version of the Child Behavior Profile.* Burlington: University of Vermont.

Edelbrock, C., Costello, A. J., Dulcan, M. K., Kalas, R., & Conover, N. C. (1985). Age differences in the reliability of the psychiatric interview of the child. *Child Development, 56,* 265-275.

Edelbrock, C., Costello, A. J., & Kessler, M. D. (1984). Empirical corrobation of attention deficit disorder. *Journal of the American Academy of Child Psychiatry, 23,* 285-290.

Edelbrock, C., Greenbaum, R., & Conover, N. C. (1985). Reliability and concurrent relations between the Teacher Version of the Child Behavior Profile and the Conners Revised Teacher Rating Scale. *Journal of Abnormal Child Psychology, 13,* 295-304.

Edelbrock, C., & McLaughlin, B. (1980). Hierarchical cluster analysis using intraclass correlations: A mixture model study. *Multivariate Behavioral Research, 15,* 229-318.

Emery, R. E. (1982). Interparental conflict and the children of discord and divorce. *Psychological Bulletin, 92,* 310-330.

Epstein, S. (1983). The stability of confusion: A reply to Mischel and Peake. *Psychological Review, 90,* 179-184.

Ernhart, C. B., Graham, F. K., Eichman, P. L., Marshall, J. M., & Thurston, D. (1963). Brain injury in the preschool child: Some developmental considerations. II. Comparison of brain injured and normal children. *Psychological Monographs, 77* (573).

Evans, W. R. (1975). The Behavior Problem Checklist. Data from an inner city population. *Psychology in the Schools, 35,* 427-431.

Exner, J. E., & Weiner, I. B. (1982). *The Rorschach: A comprehensive system. Vol. 3: Assessment of children and adolescents.* New York: John Wiley.

Feingold, B. F. (1976). Hyperkinesis and learning disabilities linked to the ingestion of artificial food colors and flavors. *Journal of Learning Disabilities, 9,* 551-559.

Flavell, J. H., & Ross, L. (Eds.). (1981). *Social cognitive development: Frontiers and possible futures.* New York: Cambridge University Press.

Fleiss, J. L., Nee, J. C., & Landis, J. R. (1979). Large sample variance of kappa in the case of different sets of raters. *Psychological Bulletin, 86,* 974-977.

Ford, M. E. (1982). Social cognition and social competence in adolescence. *Developmental Psychology, 18,* 323-340.

Frankenburg, W. K., & Dodds, J. B. (1968). *The Denver Developmental Screening Test Manual.* Denver: University of Colorado Press.

Freedman, B. J., Rosenthal, L., Donahoe, C. P., Schlundt, D. G., & McFall, R. M. (1978). A social-behavioral analysis of skill deficits in delinquent and nondelinquent adolescent boys. *Journal of Consulting and Clinical Psychology, 46,* 1448-1462.

Freeman, M. (1971). A reliability study of psychiatric diagnosis in childhood and adolescence. *Journal of Child Psychology and Psychiatry, 12,* 42-54.

Freud, A. (1936). *The ego and the mechanisms of defense.* New York: International Universities Press.

Freud, A. (1965). *Normality and pathology in childhood.* New York: International Universities Press.

Freud, A. (1980). Child analysis as the study of mental growth. In S. E. Greenspan & G. H. Pollock (Eds.), *The course of life: Psychoanalytic contributions toward understanding personality development. Vol. I: Infancy and early childhood.* Adelphi, MD: NIMH Mental Health Study Center.

Freud, S. (1900). The interpretation of dreams. In *Standard edition of the complete psychological works of Sigmund Freud* (Vol. 4). London: Hogarth Press.

Freud, S. (1926). Inhibition, symptoms, and anxiety. In *Standard edition of the complete psychological works of Sigmund Freud* (Vol. 20). London: Hogarth Press.

Freud, S. (1932). The acquisition of power over fire. *International Journal of Psycho Analysis, 8,* 405-410.

Friedlander, M. L., & Phillips, S. D. (1984). Preventing errors in clinical judgment. *Journal of Consulting and Clinical Psychology, 52,* 366-371.

Frommer, E. A. (1967). Treatment of childhood depression with antidepressant drugs. *British Medical Journal, 1,* 729-732.

Garduk, E. L., & Haggard, E. A. (1972). Immediate effects on patients of psychoanalytic interpretations. *Psychological Issues, 7* (28).

Gittelman, R. (1980). The role of psychological tests for differential diagnosis in child psychiatry. *Journal of the American Academy of Child Psychiatry, 19,* 413-438.

Gittelman, R. (1982). Prospective follow-up study of hyperactive children. Presented at the American Academy of Child Psychiatry, Washington, D. C.

Glennon, B., & Weisz, J. R. (1978). An observational approach to the assessment of anxiety in young children. *Journal of Consulting and Clinical Psychology, 46,* 1246-1257.

Gould, M. S., Shaffer, D., & Rutter, M. (1985). UK/WHO Study of ICD-9. (unpublished)

Greene, R. L. (1978). Can clients provide valuable feedback to clinicians about their personality interpretation? Green replies. *Journal of Consulting and Clinical Psychology, 46,* 1496-1497.

Greenspan, S. I., Hatleberg, J. L., & Cullander, C.C.H. (1980). A developmental approach to systematic personality assessment: Illustrated with the case of a 6-year-old child. In S. I. Greenspan & G. Pollock (Eds.), *The course of life: Psychoanalytic contributions toward understanding personality development. Vol. II: Latency, adolescence, and youth.* Washington, DC: DHEW.

Griesinger, W. (1867). *Mental pathology and therapeutics.* C. L. Robertson & J. Rutherford (Trans). London: New Sydenham Society. (Original pub. 1845)

Group for the Advancement of Psychiatry (1966). Psychopathological disorders in childhood: Theoretical considerations and a proposed classification. *Report 62.* New York: Author.

Guzé, S. (1978). Validating criteria for psychiatric diagnosis: The Washington University approach. In M. S. Akiskal & W. L. Webb (Eds.), *Psychiatric diagnosis: Exploration of biological predictors.* New York: Spectrum.

Harder, D. W., Strauss, J. S., Kokes, R. F., Ritzler, B. A., & Gift, T. E. (1980). Life events and psychopathology severity among first psychiatric admissions. *Journal of Abnormal Psychology, 89,* 165-180.

Hartmann, D. P. (1977). Considerations in the choice of interobserver reliability estimates. *Journal of Applied Behavior Analysis, 10,* 103-116.

Hartmann, D. P. (1983). Editorial. *Behavioral Assessment, 5,* 1-3.

Hathaway, S. R., & McKinley, J. C. (1943). *The Minnesota Multiphasic Personality Schedule.* Minneapolis: University of Minnesota Press.

Hayvren, M., & Hymel, S. (1984). Ethical issues in sociometric testing: Impact of sociometric measures on interactive behavior. *Developmental Psychology, 20,* 844-849.

Heath, G. A., Hardesty, V. A., & Goldfine, P. E. (1984). Firesetting, enuresis, and animal cruelty. *Child and Adolescent Psychotherapy, 1,* 97-100.

Heath, G. A., Hardesty, V. A., Goldfine, P. E., & Walker, A. M. (1983). Childhood firesetting: An empirical study. *Journal of the American Academy of Child Psychiatry, 22,* 370-374.

Hetherington, E. M., & Martin, B. (1979). Family interaction. In H. C. Quay & J. S. Werry (Eds.), *Psychopathological disorders of childhood* (2nd ed.). New York: John Wiley.

Hobbs, N. (1975). *Issues in the classification of children.* San Francisco: Jossey-Bass.

Hodges, K., McKnew, D., Cytryn, L., Stern, L., & Kline, J. (1982). The Child Assessment Schedule (CAS) diagnostic interview: A report on reliability and validity. *Journal of the American Academy of Child Psychiatry, 21,* 468-473.

Horowitz, L. M., Post, D. L., French, R. deS., Wallis, K. D., & Siegelman, E. Y. (1981). The prototype as a construct in abnormal psychology: 2. clarifying disagreement in psychiatric judgments. *Journal of Abnormal Psychology, 90,* 575-585.

Horowitz, L. M., Wright, J. C., Lowenstein, E., & Parad, H. W. (1981). The prototype as a construct in abnormal psychology: 1. A method for deriving prototypes. *Journal of Abnormal Psychology, 90,* 568-574.

Hyler, S. E., Williams, J.B.W., & Spitzer, R. L. (1982) Reliability in the *DSM*-III field trials: Interview v case summary. *Archives of General Psychiatry, 39,* 1275-1278.

Ireton, H., & Thwing, E. J. (1974). *Minnesota Child Development Inventory.* Minneapolis: Behavior Science Systems.

Jenkins, R. L., & Boyer, A. (1968). Types of delinquent behavior and background factors. *International Journal of Social Psychiatry, 14,* 65-76.

Jenkins, R. L., & Glickman, S. (1946). Common syndromes in child psychiatry: I. Deviant behavior traits. II. The schizoid child. *American Journal of Orthopsychiatry, 16,* 244-261.

Jones, M. C. (1924). A laboratory study of fear: The case of Peter. *Pedagogical Seminary, 31,* 308-315.

Kahn, E. (1959). Emil Kraepelin. In B. Pasaminick (Ed.), *Epidemiology of mental disorders.* Washington, DC: American Association for Advancement of Science.

Kahneman, D., Slovic, P., & Tversky, A. (Eds.). (1982). *Judgment under uncertainty: Heuristics and biases.* Cambridge, England: Cambridge University Press.

Kanner, L. (1943). Autistic disturbances of affective contact. *Nervous Child, 2,* 217-250.

Kasanin, J., & Kaufman, M. R. (1929). A study of the functional psychoses in childhood. *American Journal of Psychiatry, 9,* 307-384.

Kashani, J. M., Husain, A., Shekim, W. O., Hodges, K. K., Cytryn, L., & McKnew, D. H. (1981). Current perspectives on childhood depression: An overview. *American Journal of Psychiatry, 138,* 143-153.

Kaufman, A. S., & Kaufman, N. L. (1983). *Kaufman Assessment Battery for Children,* Circle Pines, MN: American Guidance Service.

Kazdin, A. E. (1979). Situational specificity: The two-edged sword of behavioral assessment. *Behavioral Assessment, 1*, 57-75.

Kazdin, A. E. (1983). Psychiatric diagnosis, dimensions of dysfunction and child behavior therapy. *Behavior Therapy, 14*, 73-99.

Kazdin, A. E. (1985). Selection of target behaviors: The relationship of the treatment focus to clinical dysfunction. *Behavioral Assessment, 7*, 33-47.

Kestenbaum, C. J., & Bird, H. R. (1978). A reliability study of the Mental Health Assessment Form for school-age children. *Journal of the American Academy of Child Psychiatry, 17*, 338-347.

Kinsbourne, M., & Swanson, J. M. (1979). Models of hyperactivity. Implications for diagnosis and treatment. In R. L. Trites (Ed.), *Hyperactivity in children: Etiology, measurement, and treatment implications.* Baltimore: University Park Press.

Klee, S. H., & Garfinkel, B. D. (1984). Identification of depression in children and adolescents: The role of the dexamethasone suppression test. *Journal of the American Academy of Child Psychiatry, 23*, 410-415.

Knobloch, H., & Pasamanick, H. (Eds.). (1974). *Gesell and Amatruda's developmental diagnosis: The evaluation and management of normal and abnormal development in infancy and early childhood* (3rd ed.). New York: Harper & Row.

Kohn, M. (1977). *Social competence, symptoms, and underachievement in childhood: A longitudinal perspective.* New York: John Wiley.

Koppitz, E. M. (1968). *Psychological evaluation of children's human figure drawings.* New York: Grune & Stratton.

Koppitz, E. M. (1975). *The Bender Gestalt Test for young children* (Vol. II). New York: Grune & Stratton.

Kovacs, M. (1981). Rating scales to assess depression in school-aged children. *Acta Paedopsychiatrica, 46*, 305-315.

Kovacs, M., & Beck, A. T. (1977). An empirical-clinical approach toward a definition of childhood depression. In J. G. Schulterbrandt & A. Raskin (Eds.), *Depression in childhood: Diagnosis, treatment, and conceptual models.* New York: Raven Press.

Kovacs, M., Feinberg, T. L., Crouse-Novak, M. A., Paulauskas, S. L., & Finkelstein, R. (1984). Depressive disorders in childhood. I. A longitudinal prospective study of characteristics and recovery. *Archives of General Psychiatry, 41*, 229-237.

Kovacs, M., Feinberg, T. L., Crouse-Novak, M., Paulauskas, S. L., Pollock, M., & Finkelstein, R. (1984). Depressive disorders in childhood. II. A longitudinal study of the risk for a subsequent major depression. *Archives of General Psychiatry, 41*, 643-649.

Kraepelin, E. (1883). *Psychiatrie* (1st ed.). Leipzig: Abel.

Kraepelin, E. (1915). *Psychiatrie* (8th ed.). Leipzig: Barth.

Kuhlmann, F. (1912). The Binet and Simon tests of intelligence in grading feebleminded children. *Journal of Psycho-asthenics, 16*, 173-193.

Kuhn, T. S. (1970). *The structure of scientific revolutions* (2nd ed.) Chicago: University of Chicago Press.

Kuhn, T. S. (1977). *The essential tension.* Chicago: University of Chicago Press.

Kuhnley, E. J., Hendren, R. L., & Quinlan, D. M. (1982). Fire-setting by children. *Journal of the American Academy of Child Psychiatry, 21*, 560-563.

Kurtz, R. M., & Garfield, S. L. (1978). Illusory correlation: A further exploration of Chapman's paradigm. *Journal of Consulting and Clinical Psychology, 46*, 1009-1015.

Lachar, D., & Gdowski, C. L. (1979). *Actuarial assessment of child and adolescent personality: An interpretive guide for the Personality Inventory for Children Profile.* Los Angeles: Western Psychological Services.

Langhorne, J., & Loney, J. (1979). A four-fold model for subgrouping the Hyperkinetic/
    MBD Syndrome. *Child Psychiatry and Human Development, 9,* 153-159.
Langner, T. S., Gersten, J. C., & Eisenberg, J. G. (1974). Approaches to measurement and
    definition in the epidemiology of behavior disorders: Ethnic background and child
    behavior. *International Journal of Health Services, 4,* 483-501.
Lefkowitz, M. M., & Tesiny, E. P. (1980). Assessment of childhood depression. *Journal of
    Consulting and Clinical Psychology, 48,* 43-50.
Lejeune, J., Gautier, M., & Turpin, R. (1963). Study of the somatic chromosomes of nine
    mongoloid idiot children. In S. H. Boyer (Ed.), *Papers on human genetics.* Englewood
    Cliffs, NJ: Prentice-Hall. (Original pub. 1959)
Lessing, E. E., Williams, V., & Revelle, W. (1981). Parallel forms of the IJR Behavior
    Checklist for parents, teachers, and clinicians. *Journal of Consulting and Clinical
    Psychology, 49,* 34-50.
Levin, D. A. (1979). The nature of the plant species. *Science, 204,* 381-384.
Lewis, J. M., Beavers, W. R., Gossett, J. T., & Phillips, V. A. (1976). *No single thread:
    Psychological health in family systems.* New York: Brunner/Mazel.
Lief, A. (1948). *The commonsense psychiatry of Dr. Adolf Meyer.* New York:
    McGraw-Hill.
Loeber, R. (1982). The stability of antisocial and delinquent child behavior: A review.
    Child Development, 53, 1431-1446.
Loney, J., Kramer, J., & Milich, R. (1981). The hyperkinetic child grows up: Predictors of
    symptoms, delinquency, and achievement at follow-up. In K. Gadow & J. Loney
    (Eds.), *Psychosocial aspects of drug treatment for hyperactivity.* Boulder, CO: West-
    view Press.
Loney, J., Whaley-Klahn, M. A., Kosier, T., & Conboy, J. (1983). Hyperactive boys and
    their brothers at 21: Predictors of aggressive and antisocial outcomes. In K. T. Van
    Dusen & S. A. Mednick (Eds.), *Prospective studies of crime and delinquency.* Boston:
    Kluwer-Nijhoff.
Lubin, B., Larsen, R. M., & Matarazzo, J. D. (1984). Patterns of psychological test use in
    the United States: 1935-1982. *American Psychologist, 32,* 451-454.
Marks, P. A., Seeman, W., & Haller, D. L. (1974). *The actuarial use of the MMPI with
    adolescents and adults.* Baltimore: Williams & Wilkins.
Mash, E. J. (1985). Some comments on target selection in behavior therapy. *Behavioral
    Assessment, 7,* 63-78.
Mash, E. J., & Terdal, L. G. (Eds.). (1981). *Behavioral assessment of childhood disorders.*
    New York: Guilford Press.
Matarazzo, J. D. (1983). Computerized psychological testing. *Science, 221,* 323.
Mattison, R., Cantwell, D. P., Russell, A. T., & Will, L. (1979). A comparison of *DSM*-II
    and *DSM*-III in the diagnosis of childhood psychiatric disorders. *Archives of General
    Psychiatry, 36,* 1217-1222.
McCarthy, D. (1972). *McCarthy Scales of Children's Abilities.* New York: Psychological
    Corporation.
McConaughy, S. M., & Ritter, D. R. (1985). Social competence and behavioral problems
    of learning disabled boys aged 6-11. *Journal of Learning Disability,* in press.
McFall, R. M. (1982). A review and reformulation of the concept of social skills. *Behavior-
    al Assessment, 4,* 1-33.
McNamara, J. R., & Blumler, C. A. (1982). Role playing to assess social competence:
    Ecological validity considerations. *Behavior Modification, 6,* 519-548.
Meehl, P. E. (1954). *Clinical versus statistical prediction.* Minneapolis: University of
    Minnesota Press.
Meehl, P. E., & Golden, R. R. (1982). Taxometric methods. In P. C. Kendall & J. N.
    Butcher (Eds.), *Handbook of research methods in clinical psychology.* New York:
    John Wiley.

Mezzich, A. C., & Mezzich, J. E. (1979, September). Diagnostic reliability of childhood and adolescent behavior disorders. Presented at American Psychological Association, New York.

Mikkelsen, E. J., Brown, G. L., Minichiello, M. D., Millican, F. K., & Rapoport, J. L. (1982). Neurologic status in hyperactive, enuretic, encopretic, and normal boys. *Journal of the American Academy of Child Psychiatry, 21,* 75-81.

Milich, R. (1984). Cross-sectional and longitudinal observations of activity level and sustained attention in a normative sample. *Journal of Abnormal Child Psychology, 12,* 261-275.

Milich, R., & Landau, S. (1984). A comparison of the social status and social behavior of aggressive and aggressive/withdrawn boys. *Journal of Abnormal Child Psychology, 12,* 277-288.

Milich, R., Loney, J., & Landau, S. (1982). Independent dimensions of hyperactivity and aggression: A validation with playroom observation data. *Journal of Abnormal Psychology, 91,* 183-198.

Milich, R., Roberts, M., Loney, J., & Caputo, J. (1980). Differentiating practice effects and statistical regression on the Conners Hyperkinesis Index. *Journal of Abnormal Child Psychology, 8,* 549-552.

Miller, L. C. (1967). Louisville Behavior Checklist for males, 6-12 years of age. *Psychological Reports, 21,* 885-896.

Miller, L. C. (1972). School Behavior Checklist: An inventory of deviant behavior for elementary school children. *Journal of Consulting and Clinical Psychology, 38,* 134-144.

Miller, L. C. (1981). *Louisville Behavior Checklist Manual.* Los Angeles: Western Psychological Services.

Mischel, W. (1979). On the interface of cognition and personality. Beyond the person-situation debate. *American Psychologist, 34,* 740-754.

Mischel, W., & Peake, P. K. (1982). Beyond deja vu in the search for cross-situational consistency. *Psychological Review, 89,* 730-755.

Montenegro, H. (1983). *Salud mental del escolar. Estandarizacion del inventario de problemas conductuales y destrezas sociales de T. Achenbach en ninos de 6 a 11 anos.* Santiago, Chile: Centro de Estudios de Desarollo y Estimulacion Psicosocial.

Moos, R. H., Clayton, J., & Max, W. (1984). *The social climate scales annotated bibliography update 1979-1983.* Palo Alto, CA: Consulting Psychologists Press.

Moos, R. H., & Fuhr, R. (1982). The clinical use of social-ecological concepts: The case of an adolescent girl. *American Journal of Orthopsychiatry, 52,* 111-122.

Moos, R. H., & Moos, B. S. (1976). A typology of family social environments. *Family Process, 15,* 357-371.

Moos, R. H. & Moos, B. (1981). *Family environment scale manual.* Palo Alto, CA: Consulting Psychologists Press.

Murray, H. A. (1943). *Thematic apperception test.* Cambridge, MA: Harvard University Press.

Mussen, P. H. (Ed.). (1983). *Handbook of child psychology* (4th ed.). New York: John Wiley.

Nagi, S. Z. (1980). A bureaucratic environment and gatekeeping decisions. In S. Salzinger, J. Antrobus, & J. Glick (Eds.), *The ecosystem of the "sick" child.* New York: Academic Press.

Nay, W. R. (1979). *Multimethod clinical assessments.* New York: Gardner Press.

Nelson, R. O. (1983). Past, present, and future. *Behavioral Assessment, 5,* 195-206.

Nisbett, R. E., Zukier, H., & Lemley, R. E. (1981). The dilution effect: Nondiagnostic information weakens the implications of diagnostic information. *Cognitive Psychology, 13,* 248-277.

Ochroch, R. (1981). *The diagnosis and treatment of minimal brain dysfunction in children. A clinical approach.* New York: Human Sciences Press.

Olweus, D. (1979). Stability of aggressive reaction patterns in males: A review. *Psychological Bulletin, 86,* 852-875.

Olweus, D., Mattson, A., Schalling, D., & Löw, H. (1980). Testosterone, aggression, physical and personality dimensions in normal adolescents. *Psychosomatic Medicine, 42,* 253-269.

Oskamp, S. (1965). Overconfidence in case-study judgments. *Journal of Consulting Psychology, 29,* 261-265.

Overall, J. E., & Hollister, L. E. (1979). Comparative evaluation of research diagnostic criteria for schizophrenia. *Archives of General Psychiatry, 36,* 1198-1205.

Patterson, G. R. (1980). Mothers: The unacknowledged victims: *Monographs of the Society for Research in Child Development, 45* (186).

Patterson, G. R. (1981). Forward. In E. J. Mash & L. G. Terdal (Eds.), *Behavioral assessment of childhood disorders.* New York: Guilford.

Pelham, W. E., Atkins, M. S., Murphy, H. A., & White, K. S. (1981, November). Operationalization and validation of attention deficit disorders. Presented at the Association for the Advancement of Behavior Therapy, Toronto.

Prior, M., Perry, D., & Gajzago, C. (1975). Kanner's syndrome of early-onset psychosis: A taxonomic analysis of 142 cases. *Journal of Autism and Childhood Schizophrenia, 5,* 71-80.

Putallaz, M. (1983). Predicting children's sociometric status from their behavior. *Child Development, 54,* 1417-1426.

Quay, H. C. (1979). Classification. In H. C. Quay & J. S. Werry (Eds.), *Psychopathological disorders of childhood* (2nd ed.). New York: John Wiley.

Quay, H. C. (1979). Residential treatment. In H. C. Quay & J. Werry (Eds.), *Psychopathological disorders of childhood* (2nd ed.). New York: John Wiley.

Reed, M., & Edelbrock, C. (1983). Reliability and validity of the Direct Observation Form of the Child Behavior Checklist. *Journal of Abnormal Child Psychology, 11,* 521-530.

Remschmidt, H. (1985). Multiaxial classification in child psychiatry. (unpublished)

Reynolds, C. R., & Paget, K. D. (1981). Factor analysis of the Revised Children's Manifest Anxiety Scale for blacks, whites, males and females with a national normative sample. *Journal of Consulting and Clinical Psychology, 44,* 352-359.

Robins, L. N. (1974). *Deviant children grown up* (2nd ed.). Huntington, NY: Krieger.

Robins, L. N., & Ratcliff, K. S. (1979). Risk factors in the continuation of childhood antisocial behavior into adulthood. *International Journal of Mental Health, 7,* 96-116.

Roff, J. D., & Wirt, R. D. (1984). Childhood aggression and social adjustment as antecedents of delinquency. *Journal of Abnormal Child Psychology, 12,* 111-126.

Rosch, E., (1978). Principles of categorization. In E. Rosch & B. B. Lloyd (Eds.), *Cognition and categorization.* Hillsdale, NJ: Erlbaum.

Rosch, E., & Mervis, C. B. (1975). Family resemblances: Studies in the internal structure of categories. *Cognitive Psychology, 7,* 573-605.

Rosch, E., Mervis, C. B., Gray, W. E., Johnson, D. M., & Boyes-Graem, P. (1976). Basic objects in natural categories. *Cognitive Psychology, 8,* 382-439.

Rosen, B. M., Bahn, A. K., & Kramer, M. (1974). Demographic and diagnostic characteristics of psychiatric clinic outpatients in the U.S.A., 1961. *American Journal of Orthopsychiatry, 34,* 455-468.

Rotter, J., & Rafferty, J. (1958). *Manual for the Rotter Incomplete Sentence Blank*. New York: Psychological Corporation.

Rushton, J. P., Brainerd, C. J., & Pressley, M. (1983). Behavioral development and construct validity: The principle of aggregation. *Psychological Bulletin, 94*, 18-38.

Rutter, M., & Giller, H. (1983). *Juvenile delinquency. Trends and prospects*. New York: Penguin.

Rutter, M., & Shaffer, D. (1980). *DSM*-III. A step forward or back in terms of the classfication of child psychiatric disorders? *Journal of the American Academy of Child Psychiatry, 19*, 371-394.

Rutter, M., Shaffer, D., & Shepherd, M. (1975). *A multiaxial classification of child psychiatric disorders. An evaluation of a proposal*. Geneva: World Health Organization.

Salzinger, S., Antrobus, J., & Glick, J. (Eds.). (1980). *The ecosystem of the "sick" child*. New York: Academic Press.

Sarason, S. B., & Klaber, M. (1985). The school as a social situation. *Annual Review of Psychology, 36*, 115-140.

Schopler, E., & Loftin, J. (1969). Thinking disorders in parents of young psychotic children. *Journal of Abnormal Psychology, 74*, 281-287.

Seidenberg, M., Giordani, B., Berent, S., & Boll, T. J. (1983). IQ level and performance on the Halstead-Reitan Neuropsychological Test Battery for older children. *Journal of Consulting and Clinical Psychology, 51*, 406-413.

Shapiro, R. J., & Budman, S. H. (1973). Defection, termination and continuation in family and individual therapy. *Family Process, 12*, 55-67.

Sharp, S. E. (1898). Individual psychology: A study in psychological method. *American Journal of Psychology, 10*, 329-391.

Siegel, L. S. (1982). Reproductive, perinatal, and environmental factors as predictors of the cognitive and language development of preterm and fullterm infants. *Child Development, 53*, 963-973.

Sleator, E. K., Ullmann, R. K., & von Neumann, A. (1982). How do hyperactive children feel about taking stimulants and will they tell the doctor? *Clinical Pediatrics, 21*, 474-479.

Smith, E. E. (1978). Theories of semantic memory. In W. K. Estes (Ed.), *Handbook of learning and cognitive processes* (Vol. 5). Hillsdale, NJ: Erlbaum.

Sneath, P.H.A., & Sokal, R. R. (1973). *Numerical taxonomy: The principles and practice of numerical classification*. San Francisco: Freeman.

Sparrow, S., Cicchetti, D. V., & Balla, D. (1984). *Vineland Social Maturity Scale-revised*. Circle Pines, MN: American Guidance Service.

Spielberger, C. D. (1973). *Preliminary test manual for the State-Trait Anxiety Inventory for Children*. Palo Alto, CA: Consulting Psychologists Press.

Spitzer, R. L., & Cantwell, D. P. (1980). The *DSM*-III classification of the psychiatric disorders of infancy, childhood, and adolescence. *Journal of the American Academy of Child Psychiatry, 19*, 356-370.

Spivak, G., & Shure, M. B. (1982). The cognition of social adjustment. In B. B. Lahey & A. E. Kazdin (Eds.), *Advances in clinical child psychology* (Vol. 5). New York: Plenum.

Stouthamer-Loeber, M., & Peters, R. DeV. (1984). A priori classification systems of observation data: The eye of the beholder. *Behavioral Assessment, 6*, 275-282.

Strauss, A. A., & Lehtinen, L. E. (1947). *Psychopathology and education of the brain-injured child*. New York: Grune & Stratton.

Strober, M., Green, J., & Carlson, G. (1981). The reliability of psychiatric diagnosis in hospitalized adolescents: Interater agreement using the *DSM*-III. *Archives of General Psychiatry, 38*, 141-145.

Swan, G. E., & MacDonald, M. L. (1978). Behavior therapy in practice: A national survey of behavior therapists. *Behavior Therapy, 9,* 799-807.

Taylor, J. J., & Achenbach, T. M. (1975). Moral and cognitive development in retarded and non-retarded children. *American Journal of Mental Deficiency, 80,* 43-50.

Terman, L. M., & Merrill, M. A. (1973). *Stanford-Binet Intelligence Scale. Manual for the third revision.* Boston: Houghton-Mifflin.

Tesiny, E. P., & Lefkowitz, M. M. (1982). Childhood depression: A 6-month follow-up study. *Journal of Consulting and Clinical Psychology, 50,* 778-780.

Trites, R., Ferguson, B., & Tryphonas, H. (1978, August). Food allergies and hyperactivity. Presented at American Psychological Association, Toronto, Ontario.

Tuber, S. (1983). Children's Rorschach scores as predictors of later adjustment. *Journal of Consulting and Clinical Psychology, 51,* 379-385.

Turkington, C. (1984). The growing use, and abuse, of computer testing. *APA Monitor, 15,* 7, 26.

Tversky, A., & Kahneman, D. (1974). Judgment under uncertainty: Heuristics and biases. *Science, 185,* 1124-1131.

Uzgiris, I. C., & Hunt, J. McV. (1975). *Assessment in infancy: Ordinal scales of psychological development.* Urbana: University of Illinois Press.

Verhulst, F. (1985). A Dutch epidemiological study using the Achenbach Child Behavior Checklist. Rotterdam, Holland: University of Rotterdam.

Wade, T. C., Baker, T. B., & Hartmann, D. T. (1979). Behavior therapists' self-reported views and practices. *Behavior Therapist, 2,* 3-6.

Wahler, R. G., Berland, R. M., & Coe, T. D. (1979). Generalization processes in child behavior change. In B. B. Lahey & A. E. Kazdin (Eds.), *Advances in clinical child psychology* (Vol. 2). New York: Plenum Press.

Wahler, R. G., & Fox, J. J. (1980). Solitary toy play and time out: A family treatment package for children with aggressive and oppositional behavior. *Journal of Applied Behavior Analysis, 13,* 23-39.

Walker, H. M. & Hops, H. (1976). Use of normative peer data as a standard for evaluating classroom treatment effects. *Journal of Applied Behavior Analysis, 9,* 159-168.

Walker, H. M., & Rankin, R. (1983). Assessing the behavioral expectations and demands of less restrictive settings. *School Psychology Review, 12,* 274-284.

Waters, E., & Sroufe, L. A. (1983). Social competence as a developmental construct. *Developmental Review, 3,* 72-87.

Watson, J. B. (1913). Pscyhology as the behaviorist views it. *Psychological Review, 20,* 158-177.

Watson, J. B., & Rayner R. (1920). Conditioned emotional reactions. *Journal of Experimental Psychology, 3,* 1-14.

Wechsler, D. (1974). *Wechsler Intelligence Scale for Children-revised.* New York: Psychological Corporation.

Wechsler, D. (1981). *Wechsler Adult Intelligence Scale-revised.* New York: Psychological Corporation.

Weinberg, W. A., Rutman, J., Sullivan, L., Penick, E. C., & Dietz, S. G. (1973). Depression in children referred to an educational diagnostic center: Diagnosis and treatment. *Journal of Pediatrics, 83,* 1065-1072.

Weisz, J. R., O'Neill, P., & O'Neill, P. C. (1975). Field dependence-independence on the Children's Embedded Figures Test: Cognitive style or cognitive level? *Developmental Psychology, 11,* 539-540.

Wender, P., & Wender, E. (1978). *The hyperactive child and the learning disabled child.* New York: Crown.

Werry, J. S., Methven, R. J., Fitzpatrick, J., & Dixon, H. (1983). The interrater reliability of *DSM*-III in children. *Journal of Abnormal Child Psychology, 11,* 341-354.

Wiggins, J. S. (1981). Clinical and statistical prediction: Where are we and where do we go from here? *Clinical Psychology Review, 1,* 3-18.

Wirt, R. D., & Broen, W. E. (1958). *Booklet for the Personality Inventory for Children.* Minneapolis: Authors.

Wirt, R. D., Lachar, D., Klinedinst, J. K., & Seat, P. D. (1977). *Multidimensional description of child personality. A manual for the Personality Inventory for Children.* Los Angeles: Western Psychological Services.

Wissler, C. (1901). The correlation of mental and physical tests. *Psychological Monographs, 3,* No. 6.

Wolpe, J. (1958). *Psychotherapy by reciprocal inhibition.* Stanford, CA: Stanford University Press.

Woodcock, R. E., & Johnson, M. B. (1977). *Woodcock-Johnson Psychoeducational Battery.* Hingham, MA: Teaching Resources Corp.

Woolf, H. B. (Ed.). (1977). *Webster's new collegiate dictionary,* Springfield, MA: Merriam.

World Health Organization (1978). *Mental disorders: Glossary and guide to their classification in accordance with the ninth revision of the international classification of diseases.* Geneva: Author.

Yorke, C. (1980). The contributions of the Diagnostic Profile and the assessment of developmental lines to child psychiatry. *Psychiatric Clinics of North America, 3,* 593-603.

Zentall, S. S., & Zentall, T. R. (1983). Optimal stimulation: A model of disordered activity and performance in normal and deviant children. *Psychological Bulletin, 94,* 446-471.

Zucker, K. J., Finegan, J. K., Doering, R. W., & Bradley, S. J. (1983). Human figure drawings of gender-problem children: A comparison to sibling, psychiatric, and normal controls. *Journal of Abnormal Child Psychology, 11,* 287-298.

NAME INDEX

194

SUBJECT INDEX

ABOUT THE AUTHOR

Thomas M. Achenbach, Professor of Psychiatry and Psychology, is Director of the Center for Children, Youth, and Families at the University of Vermont Department of Psychiatry. A graduate of Yale, he received his Ph.D. from the University of Minnesota and was a Postdoctoral Fellow at the Yale Child Study Center. Before moving to the University of Vermont, he taught at Yale and was a Research Psychologist at the National Institute of Mental Health. He has been a DAAD Fellow at the University of Heidelberg, Germany, an SSRC Senior Faculty Fellow at Jean Piaget's Centre d'Epistémologie Génétique in Geneva, Chair of the American Psychological Association's Task Force on Classification of Children's Behavior, and a consultant to the American Psychiatric Association's Workgroup to Revise *DSM*-III. He is the author of *Developmental Psychopathology, Research in Developmental Psychology: Concepts, Strategies, Methods,* and (with Craig Edelbrock) *The Manual for the Child Behavior Checklist and Revised Child Behavior Profile.*